Percy Fitzgerald

Eucharistic Jewels

For Persons Living in the World

Percy Fitzgerald

Eucharistic Jewels
For Persons Living in the World

ISBN/EAN: 9783743426320

Manufactured in Europe, USA, Canada, Australia, Japa

Cover: Foto ©Lupo / pixelio.de

Manufactured and distributed by brebook publishing software (www.brebook.com)

Percy Fitzgerald

Eucharistic Jewels

EUCHARISTIC JEWELS

FOR PERSONS LIVING IN THE WORLD

BY

PERCY FITZGERALD, M.A., F.S.A.

Panem de cœlo præstitisti eis: omne delectamentum in se habentem

LONDON: BURNS & OATES, Limited
NEW YORK: CATHOLIC PUBLICATION SOCIETY CO.
1889

Inscribed

TO

FRANK C. BURNAND.

PREFACE.

This little Cento will be found to contain many choice and possibly unfamiliar passages selected from the best sources. *Je prends mon bien où je le trouve*, Molière's plea, is more justifiable in the case of a religious book than in any other.

I may add that Father Bridgett has been kind enough to read over my own contributions to these pages.

ATHENÆUM CLUB,
December, 1888.

EUCHARISTIC JEWELS.

I.

The Tabernacle.

'WHAT do I behold here?' exclaims Lavater in a fine passage, when describing his emotions in a church. 'Does not everything under these majestic vaults speak to me of Thee? This cross, this golden image, is it not made for Thy honour? The censers which wave round the priest, the *Gloria* sung in choirs, the beautiful light of the perpetual lamp, these lighted tapers,—all is done for Thee. Why is the Host elevated, if it be not to honour Thee, O Jesus Christ, who art dead for love of us; because it is no more, and Thou art it, the believing Church bends the knee. It is in Thy honour that these children, early instructed, make the sign of the cross, and their tongues sing Thy praise, that they strike their breasts thrice with their little hands! It is for love of Thee that one kisses the spot which bears Thy adorable Blood. The riches collected from distant countries, the magnificence of chasubles,—all have relation to Thee! Why are the walls and the high altar of marble clothed with verdant tapestry on the day of the Blessed Sacrament? For whom do they make a road of flowers? For whom are these banners embroidered? These bells, within a thousand towers, purchased with the gold of whole cities, do they not bear Thy image cast in the very mould? Is it not for Thee they send forth their solemn tone? O delightful rapture, Jesus Christ, for Thy disciple to trace the marks of Thy finger where the eyes of the world see them not! O joy ineffable for souls devoted to Thee, to behold in caves and on rocks, and in every crucifix placed upon hills, and upon highways, Thy seal, and that of Thy love!'

One of these old fanes, say in a foreign land where the Tabernacle is enshrined, its vast aisles stretching away in shadows and recesses, its doors open always, has as many associations as an old city. Generations have passed by it and passed away; in it have their souls lived and found peace; its walls and columns are, as it were, encrusted and enriched with prayers, aspirations, holy thoughts, and memorials; every little chapel, every corner and recess, has its store of accumulated piety; while the melodious old organ perched aloft on the Rood, like the stern of some old Spanish galleon, jangling out its wheezy harmonies, has swelled and trembled a thousand times, as it led the hymns and masses. A church thus enriched with the pious accumulations of centuries, nay, the smallest, rudest building, into which we enter on a country walk, seems to be furnished at every turn and corner with suggestive things, owing to the eternal spirit of life which is there enthroned. With this feeling we may contrast the curious chilling barrenness which reigns in other temples, and which seems to suggest little more than some convenient place of meeting.

'There,' says the learned and pious author of *Mores Catholici*, 'in those vast basilicas, thronged with innumerable people upon a festal day, amid the splendour of the saints, one might avoid all notice, and feel himself solitary and unobserved. There, before the sacramental presence, the poor stranger, forgotten and forsaken in a foreign land, alone in the crowd, beholds his one, ancient, and only constant friend—the friend of his childhood, the friend of his youth, his friend for eternity. There, too, you will sometimes remark the timid maiden, or some child that recalls the image of a divine prototype, who, stealing from observation, drops a small piece of money upon the plate, after kissing the Cross of Christ. Oh, how mysterious and solemn a thing is it thus to be alone in the saintly crowd!—to pass, as it were, a disembodied spirit through such a host of ghostly combatants, thirsting after justice and the streams of a happier world! The land of malediction ends here. No more of its restrictions, of its conventional barriers. No one marshals you, no one heeds you. There are pillars behind which you may kneel and weep in secret. There are retired chapels in which you may lie prostrate before the Blessed Sacrament! The poor walk here free and favoured, as in presence of nature; they can approach to the altar, near as kings, and can enjoy equally with the pomp and glory of nobility the splendour and loveliness of the house of God. In the church, as St. Chrysostom says, is the common house of all men, in which one priest offers peace in common to all; and if concord were properly preserved, he adds, we should have need of no other.'

Such a scene furnishes striking reflections as to the presence of our Saviour in the throng. We too often forget that this presence is continuous; that He passed, as it were, from Jerusalem to the

Tabernacle, and has lived there for nearly nineteen hundred years; and that the scenes described in the New Testament are renewed for us every day and hour. 'You open the book of the Divine Scriptures' (goes on our author), 'and you read how Christ the Messiah walked in Judea, how He passed through the multitude, how they cried out, "Jesus, Son of God, have mercy on us". How the people thronged round, heard and adored, and you say, "How happy the eyes which saw Him, and the ears which heard His divine words!" But approach, enter the churches, the world of spirits, and exercise that faith which has the promise of life eternal; for when the mystic train moves through the prostrate multitude, while the hymn rises, you have more encouragement, nay, greater evidences to force you to adore Him, in sacramental presence, than those men possessed who saw the Infant of Bethlehem, and Jesus of Nazareth in the sorrows and humiliations of His humanity. Fall down then and adore the Messiah, and according to your faith He will have mercy on you. Are you a child of sorrow, you will be comforted; mark and obey the prophetic inspiration. "All you that thirst come to the waters, and you who have not silver, hasten, come and eat." Trust the experience of men who long like you have trod the common ways of life, and assure you that it will be so, that you will be filled with benediction, filled with joy.'

'When you see the Body of Jesus Christ upon our altars,' says St. John Chrysostom, in one of his Homilies, 'say to yourself, By this Body I am no longer dust and ashes: I am no more a slave: I am free: I can hope for heaven and all its blessings—life immortal, the company of angels, and the sight of Jesus Christ! The sun itself could not look on this Body fixed to the cross—the veil of the Temple and the rocks were rent with grief, and the while earth shook. Would you know by other instances the extent of His power, ask the woman who was healed by touching, not His Body, but His garment—and merely the hem of His garment. Ask the sea which bore Him up on its waves. Ask the demon who it is that has given him a mortal wound—destroyed his strength, made him a slave, arrested his efforts, and put him to flight! He will tell you that it is this Body which has crushed his head, and triumphed over his power. Ask of death who it is that has snatched his sting, borne away his victory, rendered him contemptible to children—death, once so terrible to kings, to the just even—it will tell you it was His Body which has wrought all these marvels.' Amazing and powerful words, to which we listen with a sort of awe.

In the same spirit, the Saint then bids us lift up our eyes to heaven, to this King of kings, '*yet Him you have upon earth*'. 'Think then, when you look upon the Eucharist, that here is the Body and Blood of Him who dwells in the highest heavens, whom angels adore, and who sits nighest the immortal and omnipotent God. But think at the same moment that you drink this Blood and eat this Body.'

This vivid sense of the reality of our Lord's presence is scarcely thought of by the average Christian. But, as a pious writer has put it, is it not true that were the simple accident of the bread removed, we should actually be as those are who stand in the great Presence? The Church and the Tabernacle would become heaven itself. It is astonishing to see how this sense of reality filled the greater saints and fathers, and what burning, convincing eloquence it lent to their tongue,.

'Who,' says St. Lawrence Justinian, developing the same thought, 'is not struck dumb with wonder at the thought that the King of glory should wish not merely to hide Himself in this mean position, but to rest in a human breast! That He should vouchsafe this favour to the just only would be much. But what shall we say when we find Him allowing the same privilege to the impious, whose treatment of Him is a continued dishonour. Once only in His life was He betrayed and sold, whereas here we find Him betrayed and sold over and over again! All the sufferings of His Passion were over in a single day; but every day at our altars He meets the same unworthy treatment. Once only He died upon the cross; but as often as Mass is said He is sacrificed.' How vividly striking and original are these words, yet they are but a simple statement of facts!

This prompts the Saint to break into the following prayer or apostrophe: 'O salutary souvenir! extraordinary sacrifice! victim infinitely acceptable to Almighty God! Bread of Life, sweet nourishment, exquisite repast, who can receive you, praise you worthily, understand you perfectly, honour you with feelings sufficiently pure, or form desires to correspond with the blessings you contain! I sink exhausted when I think of you; my tongue halts when I would speak of you; I am incapable of exalting you according to the measure of my wishes. So grant me, O my God, an enlightened spirit and an eloquent tongue to publish forth the wonders of Thy great Sacrament. For the mind of man, even all the intelligence of angels, could not suffice to comprehend and explain them.'

One of the finest bursts, worthily commensurate with the immensity of the gift, is found in the Bull of Institution of Corpus Christi—a really inspired utterance, that kindles the reader. 'In this most holy commemoration we shed tears, devoutly rejoicing; for our heart, all filled with gladness, causes our eyes to pour forth tears. O the immensity of the heavenly love! O overflowing divine piety! O most profuse liberality of our God! He had given us all things; He had conferred upon us the dominion of all creatures upon the earth; and had so exalted us as to appoint His angels to assist us, whom He has sent to minister to them who shall receive the inheritance of salvation. Though His bounty had been so great, to show it still more, out of the immense charity which He bears us, He hath given Himself to us; and, surpassing all His other liberalities, exceeding all measure of love, He gives Himself to us to be our food! O singular and admirable bounty, in which He that gives is the gift Himself! Prodigious is the liberality when anyone gives himself! He bestows Himself for our nourishment, to the end that man, who was fallen to death by one kind of food, should be raised to life by another meat. Man fell by the mortal apple, and is again raised by the food of the Tree of Life. On the one tree hung the morsel of our death; on this the nourishing of our life. The taste of that overthrew us; the taste of this saves us. Behold now whence the evil has entered, from thence has come the medicine, and from whence death sprang life has also come forth. It was said of the other meat, "The day thou eatest of it thou shalt die"; and it is said of this, "He that eats of this bread shall live for ever". O most exalted Sacrament! O most worthy to be adored, revered, glorified, honoured, exalted with the most singular praises, recommended by the loudest acclamations!'

'Who shall tell you,' says Lacordaire in one of his Conferences, 'what the love of Jesus Christ is, if you have never known it; and if you have but for a single instant tasted it, who shall recount to you its unutterable effect? Not the transports of pride in the day of its greatest triumphs, nor the fascination of the flesh in the hour of its most deceitful delights, nor the mother recovering a son from the hands of God, nor the bridegroom leading his bride, nor the poet in the first flight of his genius, nor anything that is or has been supposed, can give an image, or a shadow, or even an inkling of what the love of Jesus Christ is in a soul. *Everything else is either too much or too little.* Jesus Christ alone has the measure of our being; He alone has made of greatness, and lowliness, and strength of motion, and of life and death, a drink such as our heart yearned for without knowing it; and those who have once tasted this cup in the day of their manhood know that I speak the truth, and that it is an intoxication from which there is no recovery.'

II.

The Communicant.

As the intending communicant opens his eyes betimes, the words of the angel will occur to him appropriately, 'Arise and eat!'—a simple thought, that fills the mind with the weightiness of what is before it. This may ring profitably in the ear as we dress and take our road to the church. We can hear, also, the invitation to Zaccheus: 'Make haste and come down, for on this day I shall lodge in thy house'. Nothing indeed is more expressive of true devotion than that ever-recurring scene of the communion: a peaceful tranquillity, modesty, humility, retirement, displayed in its quintessence.

At early morning, in some tranquil church, when the busy world without is hurrying to the storm and stress of the long day, the sight of the faithful pressing forward to the railings is itself (to vary Steele's phrase) 'a pious education'. There is shown a gentle ardour, a modest approach; while the faces of those who have received are illumined with a sort of divine inspiration. 'If to behold the divine beauty of the human countenance,' says the author of *Mores Catholici*, 'be at all times sweet to minds contemplative, where can this pleasure be enjoyed so fully as in the church! Those raptures of love mixed with sorrow at the solemn moment of communion give a sublime expression to the features . . . grief almost always ennobles the countenance. The instinct of our primitive destiny seeks another dignity besides that of sorrow. The true condition of man is the reparation of his misery: this form never appears clothed in its most beautiful terrestrial, excepting when it takes the expression of this mystery of sorrow and grace, when it receives the imprint of a divine joy, penetrates to the abyss of our sufferings.'

Indeed anyone who, when serving Mass, has stood by the priest when he is administering communion, will have noted an extraordinary and edifying spectacle in the upturned faces, well-nigh transformed by an almost divine light; with, in some instances, a kind of rapt anticipation—a gentleness and patience—a look of a world beyond. The spectacle, for those who do not communicate, seems even to renew a scene from our Saviour's life. He is passing by, as if about to work a miracle. We might fancy ourselves in the streets of Jerusalem, and should seize the opportunity to call to Him with the blind man, 'Jesus, son of David, have mercy on me!' There is indeed no actual difference between the two scenes: and wise are they who embrace the opportunity and call upon the Son of man for aid and relief in their difficulty.

It is a quiet week-day morning in some unfrequented chapel where scarce half-a-dozen are present. This slender attendance may have the significance of a crowd after all in the *largeness* of devotion in a single pious heart. We may have one such soul kneeling beside us who, as it were, has stolen modestly to the railing, and returns with an edifying absorption—unconscious almost of all around her. As she drops into her place again beside us, may we reflect, with a certain awe, that we are more nearly concerned; that here is a living tabernacle that has just enshrined our Lord; and that at the moment is going on beside us, within touch almost, secret and all but divine colloquies between her Lord and the soul He has thus visited. Truly we feel this is holy ground, and if we are impressed with the sanctity of this neighbourhood we shall find in it even a more reverential form of the spiritual communion. As the Mass goes on, and the moment approaches, we may borrow from the liturgy of the Sacrifice itself those close nervous prayers which are so appropriate to our own case.

Thus after the *Pater noster*, we may recite the

Libera, or prayer for deliverance : *Deliver us, we beseech Thee, O Lord, from all evil of soul and body: and by the intercession of the Blessed Mary ever Virgin and of all the saints, mercifully grant us peace in our days, through Jesus Christ our Lord. Amen.* After this the *Agnus Dei*, addressed directly to Him who is presently to be received; and then the powerful prayer : *Lord Jesus Christ, Son of the living God, who by the will of the Father hast by Thy death given life to the world, deliver me by this, Thy most precious Body and Blood, from all my evils and all my iniquities : make me always adhere to Thy commandments, and never let me be separated from Thee. Amen.*

On approaching the rails, another passage from the early part of the Mass will suggest itself : *Take away, we beseech Thee, O Lord, our iniquities, that we may be worthy to enter with pure minds into the Holy of Holies.*

Then, too, may be repeated the words used by the celebrant : *I will take the bread of heaven and call upon the name of the Lord.* And so with the words : *Let not the taking of Thy Body, Lord Jesus Christ, which I, unworthy, presume to receive, lead me to judgment and condemnation, but out of Thy benignity may it avail to the safety of my soul and body!* Another wholesome practice is to vividly excite the imagination, and figure ourselves waiting, on the bed of death, for the arrival of the Viaticum, and fancy that it is to be our last time of receiving.

How appropriate, too, and forcible would be the prayer and versicle used at the Benediction : *Thou hast given them bread from heaven, containing within them every delight.* And this also :

O God, who, in this wondrous Sacrament, hast

left us the memory of Thy Passion: grant, we implore, that we may so venerate the sacred mysteries of Thy Body and Blood, that we may ever feel within us the fruit of Thy redemption!

The words of the priest as he holds up the ciborium are truly powerful and appropriate: *Behold the Lamb of God! Behold Him who takes away the sins of the world!* Then speaking in the name of the communicant: *Lord, I am not worthy that Thou shouldst enter under my roof; but only say the word and my soul shall be healed!*

At this moment one may well recall the scene of institution of the Sacrament. There is seen our Saviour seated at the table. His voice is heard— His who, the day before He suffered, took bread into His holy and venerable hands, and lifting up His eyes to heaven said, *This is My Body.* We, you, all, are the disciples. He is now seen drawing near.

The words used by the priest when receiving are those of the centurion when he welcomed our Lord to his house. This worthy, humble soldier never dreamed that his simple salutation was destined to be oftener repeated than any form of words known on this earth! It was, indeed, an extraordinary compliment or reward for his devotion and humility. As every morning comes round in every quarter of the globe, his humble words, *Lord, I am not worthy that thou shouldst enter under my roof; but only say the word and my soul shall be healed*, are recited millions and millions of times over, in this holy association with our Lord's presence. He has thus acquired a permanent companionship never to be interrupted on earth.

This declaration should be in the heart of everyone, and really expresses more than the longest prayer. There is the extremest humility and profound gratitude; a hope and confidence in our Lord's great goodness. There is pleading for our shortcomings; a reminder, too, of the promise, 'Ask and you shall receive'. So we repeat, 'Say but the word and my soul shall be healed'.

The words which acccompany the administration are: *The Body of our Lord Jesus Christ keep thy soul unto eternal life*—a prayer that the Lord, as He has entered, would keep close and vigilant watch over us until eternity begins.

With equal appropriateness, when all is finished, and the priest has ascended the altar, we may repeat Simeon's words: *Now, O Lord, dost Thou dismiss Thy servant in peace, for my eyes have this day seen Thy Salvation;* and there is a short prayer said by the priest as he replaces the ciborium in the Tabernacle, which may be appropriated by the communicant: *What we have taken in the mouth, O Lord, may we receive with a pure heart, and from a gift that is temporal be it to us an eternal remedy.*

Or there is a noble passage in a Homily of St. John of the Golden Mouth, which has a sort of living reality. 'When thou seest it set before thee; say thou to thyself: "Because of this Body am I no longer earth and ashes, no longer a prisoner, but free. Because of this Body, I hope for heaven, and to receive the good things therein—immortal life, the portion of angels' converse. This Body, nailed and scourged, was more than death could stand against; this Body the sun saw crucified and turned aside his beams. This is even that Body, the blood-stained, the smitten."' What thrilling words! what a majestic pealing chime! And again for the moments after communion, we may borrow his stirring words: 'And when, filled with this Sacrament, we depart into the other world, with what confidence we shall tread the sacred threshold fenced round as with a golden armour! And why speak of the world to come, since here this mystery makes earth become to thee a heaven. *Open for once only the gates of heaven, nay the heaven of heavens, and what is there, the most precious of all, this will I show thee lying upon the earth. Seest thou not that what is more precious than all things is seen by thee on earth, not seen only but touched, and not only touched but eaten.'*

It is wonderful in what a multiplied and varied development this perpetual presence of our Lord is manifested, and in how many gracious ways we are drawn to the Tabernacle. We may thus be in contact with Him, if we will, in every act and stage of our course. There is the Mass for all; the Benediction; the Corpus Christi; the Forty Hours, also for all. There is the Communion and the Viaticum for each.

Of all the services, after, of course, the Mass, the most pleasing and soothing is the one during which our Lord is drawn, as it were, from His cell and displayed to the faithful in the Benediction (the *Salut*, or 'Salutation,' as it is styled in France), a most natural and becoming and satisfactory mode of bringing the faithful face to face, as it were, with their Redeemer, to whom they can thus address personally all their supplications.*

---

* To a saintly and zealous priest, F. Olier, of St. Sulpice in Paris, we owe this ceremonial, who early in the seventeenth century established a custom of taking the Blessed Host from the Tabernacle on the first Sundays and Thursdays of each month and exposing it for a short time on the altar. Since then it has been regularly established

F. Faber has well expressed the general feeling of all who attend at the Benediction. 'I never,' he says, 'see the Blessed Sacrament without being reminded of the last judgment of the world. Its very merciful stillness is a continual admonition to me of that resonant pomp and burning majesty. When I hold it in my hands I can only feel that it is my Judge I am holding. The silence of the Blessed Sacrament seems ever to be saying, "Jesus has nothing to think of but you". And the angels say, "O happy you". And heaven envies us, and earth rejoices to bear the race of the sons of men. But our own soul, O perverse thing, how little it knows its own happiness! Look at Him in His majesty. He puts forth all His omnipotence to hinder our forgetting Him. He exhausts His infinite wisdom to prevent our hearts growing cold towards Him. He comes into our streets, lies upon our altars, causes bells to ring and thuribles to smoke.'

'How touching,' he says in another place, 'is that word *patria* at the end of the *O Salutaris*, as if the very nearness of Jesus, the very privilege of the passing moment, only deepened the sense of exile, and as if the echo of our hearts to the sight of Him in His sacramental veils could only be that word "country," so sweet to an exile's ear, so sad in an exile's mouth.'

He adds these further original suggestions: 'One Body is at one time in all Hosts, and that without extension, while His presence is multiplied through the length and breadth of the earth in Hosts almost

as an essential portion of Catholic worship, and combined with the more formal and devotional 'exposition' of the Forty Hours, which, however, is older by three-quarters of a century.

beyond number. So that, while we admire the extreme littleness to which the Eternal Word has reduced Himself, that very littleness is such an image of the divine immensity as is not to be found elsewhere in all creation.

'The frailty' (of the Host) 'is the image of God's eternity. For the bread we eat is nothing less than eternal life. We cannot break it, divide it, diminish it, corrupt it, even though we eat it. It is whole and equal in each part, and a million others eat it and will continue to eat it until the end of time, when He will still remain the bread of life and Himself be life eternal.'

And again. 'He will draw them, says He in the monstrance, with the cords of Adam, with the bands of love. Lord, we spoke of Thee as in heaven, and lo! Thou art here. Thou makest all life now like one continued walk to Emmaus. Our hearts burn, and it is not that we know not why, but that we will not remember why. The tapers have a little wasted and the flowers have a little languished, and, amid the silent throng of worshippers, He has heard many a secret of the heart, healed many a wound, answered many a petition, and accorded many a benediction. Grace is darting from Him like sunbeams from out His pure crystal palaces.'

It was a fine and ennobling idea to celebrate this Sacrament by a distinct and regular festival, which abroad is honoured by processions through the streets and tokens of public homage and praise. On these solemnities, persons of the highest distinction, including kings and princes, walked in the throng, thus conspicuously abdicating, as it were, in a greater presence. This great festival was instituted so far back as the year 1264.

St. Thomas is said to have composed the office of the Mass, given in the Breviary for this festival, which is considered to be a perfect and inspiring composition. In it is found the well-known *Lauda Sion*, and the prayer so familiar at Benediction, *Deus, qui nobis sub sacramento mirabili*. The gradual runs: 'The eyes of all hope in Thee, O Lord, and Thou givest them meat in due season. Thou openest Thy hand and fillest every living creature with Thy blessing. Thy flesh is meat indeed,' &c. The gospel is from the 6th chapter of St. John, and contains our Lord's address to the Jews. 'He that eateth My Flesh and drinketh My Blood, abideth in Me and I in him.' Indeed, a pious person would find it profitable to read over this fine office as a preparation, and it will bring before him a sort of epitome of the history and meaning of the Sacrament.

Thus, in the Mass, Communion (our own and that of others), Benediction, Exposition, and Corpus Christi, we have abundant and varied opportunities for developing our intimacy with the Sacrament. The supreme, most critical one comes at the end —'last scene of all which ends our strange eventful history'—at the moment of the Viaticum, the communion for 'the journey'. It must be a strange overpowering feeling that pause at the threshold of the next world, those few last collected instants before death stretches out his hand. No one that has lived has ever recorded or described these sensations. The very terms of the supposition—that death is there—excludes description of the sensation. Cardinal Newman, in his wonderful *Dream of Gerontius*, has held aside the dark curtain for an instant, and furnished an idea of the sinking bewilderment of those overpowering moments. We can fancy whole firmaments beginning to open on the astounded gaze:

> ''Tis this new feeling, never felt before,
> That I am going, that I am no more.
> 'Tis this strange innermost abandonment,
> This emptying out of each constituent
> And natural force, by which I come to be. . . .
> And turn no whither, but must needs decay
> And drop from out this universal frame
> Into that shapeless, scopeless, blank abyss.'

How strange that this, the commonest, most multiplied act on earth, confronting us at every turn, should be the one thing utterly unknown, and that when approached, the dark, impassable iron veil descends.

But, if this be an overpowering sensation, who shall conceive the strange mysterious sense that must attend the reception of the Viaticum, the being 'houselled,' according to the old expressive term, for the last time! Hitherto, through life, there has been that formal 'going to communion,' lightly thought of, lightly done. But to receive Him now is a different thing; then, within a few moments, it may be, to be ushered into the palace of the silent land, where He shall receive us who have just been receiving Him. We have seen and are often told of those who at this moment are edifying, full of trust, hope, and love; but there must be within all the time a flutter of emotion, a sense hitherto unknown, the idea of *reality* never before experienced.

Read by this light, how grand, and pathetic also, are the words with which the poor departing soul is sped on her way! 'Depart, Christian soul, out of this world, in the name of God, the Father Almighty, who created thee; in the name of Jesus Christ, Son of the living God, who suffered for thee; in the name of the Holy Ghost, who sanctified thee; in the name of the angels, archangels, thrones and dominations, cherubim and seraphim. I recommend thee, dear sister, to Almighty God, and leave thee to His mercy, whose creature thou art, that, having paid the common debt by surrendering thy soul, thou mayest return to thy Maker who formed thee out of the earth. Let, therefore, the holy angels meet thy soul at its departure; let the court of the Apostles receive thee; let the triumphant army of glorious martyrs conduct thee; let the crowds of joyful confessors encompass thee; let the choir of blessed virgins go before thee; and let a happy rest be thy portion in the company of the patriarchs. *Let Jesus Christ appear to thee with a mild and cheerful countenance, and give thee a place among those who are to be in His presence for ever !'* Here is heard the sound as of trumpets before the gates, and the ushering in with hope and triumph.

III.

The Holy Eucharist a Power on Earth.

But apart from the relations of the Holy Eucharist to each individual soul, there is a large, noble, and broader view of its operation as one of the vast constituent facts of the universe, whose influence, unacknowledged if it be, has direct control of the whole course of the world. Any scheme of criticism that ignores or leaves aside this supernatural factor must be false or imperfect, and might as well leave aside the Incarnation itself. It will be seen how vast and interesting a question is thus opened; and it has been touched in a sermon, short but of much significance, delivered at York by Cardinal Manning more than twenty years ago. He here seemed to develop, in a Catholic sense, Butler's masterly argument, dwelling on the strange inconsistency or philosophical blindness that ignores what is as palpable and potent as other great Christian 'epoch-making' events. As F. Faber puts it: 'All the doctrines of the Church—Creation, Incarnation, Grace, Sacraments—run up into the doctrine of the Blessed Sacrament, and are magnificently developed there. All the art and ceremonial, the liturgical wisdom, and the rubrical majesty of the Church are grouped round.'

'The presence,' the Cardinal says, 'of the Incarnate Word in the Blessed Sacrament is the basis and the centre of an order of divine facts and operations in the world. They spring from it, rest upon it, and are united to it, so that where the Blessed Sacrament is, they are; where it is not, *they cannot be.* Men believe, then, in the whole order of natural facts, because they are palpable and immutable. They believe in the succession of day and night, of seasons, tides, and growth; but they are so immersed in sense that they cannot realise that there is a higher order of divine facts and of supernatural operations more permanent, more immutable, more unerring, of which Jesus in the Blessed Sacrament is the creating and sustaining centre.'

To see the effect of this operation of our Lord's continued presence upon earth, we have only to look back and look around us. In all the changes of the world, we shall find this to be the sustaining power of one side and its irresistible force. Nor is this a mere fanciful agent to be appreciated by metaphysicians only or by pietists. 'It underlies everything, and is as distinct as Christianity itself. "By Him all things can exist." For there are faculties of appreciation rising in degree—viz., sense, reason, and faith—each having its sphere. Sense, unless misdirected, is infallible in its reports. Reason elevates and corrects sense. But faith is above both, and is expressive and infallible. Thus the few who saw our Lord by sense believed Him to be "the carpenter whose mother and sisters we know". Sense carried them no further. Nicodemus, by reason, knew him to be "a teacher sent from God, for no man could do the miracles he did, except God were with him". This was a dictate of reason. But Peter knew him by faith.

'The working of this wonderful force is to be traced back to the beginning of Christianity. There is "a perfect chain of these divine truths. His omnipotence has called into existence two creations—the old and the new, and He is always *in contact* with His works." From this contact arise five divine facts: the Creation, Incarnation, Holy Eucharist, Mystical Body, and Resurrection. This chain of divine truths the Blessed Sacrament unites as by a clasp.'

This public presence and power of our Lord is recognised to work in the most striking way; though agnostics, atheists, *e tutte quanti*, struggle hard to ignore it, it seems to be the whole Christian life, and this can be forcibly realised by striving for a moment to imagine it withdrawn, or as having never been given. But here imagination fails us; for it is of the essence of the whole scheme of life. We might as well strive to conceive of man with four senses only, or without the notions of time or space. For the Catholic believer, of course, the sense of the actual presence needs no proof.

'The Greek schism,' goes on the Cardinal, 'has valid orders. The presence of Jesus is recoverable, and one day may rise again as from the dead. Not so those bodies which have lost the perpetual presence of Jesus in the Blessed Sacrament. They are in dissolution, and must be recreated by the same divine power. For where the Blessed Sacrament is not, all dies, as when the sun departs all things sicken and decay, and when life is gone the body returns to its dust.

'Does anyone know the name of the man who removed the Blessed Sacrament from York Minster? Was it in the morning or in the evening? But a change which held both in earth and in heaven had been accomplished. The city of York went on the day after as the day before. But the Light of Life had gone out of it; there was no Holy Sacrifice offered in the Minster. The Scriptures were read there, but there was no Divine Teacher to interpret them. The *Magnificat* was chanted still, but it rolled along the empty roof, *for Jesus was no longer on the altar.* So it is till this day. There is no light, no tabernacle, no altar, nor can be, till Jesus shall return thither. It stands like the open sepulchre; and we may believe that the angels are there, ever saying, "He is not here. Come and see the place where the Lord was laid."'

So striking and original a passage as this supplies an ennobling idea of the great Sacrament, and lifts us into a new domain. Thoughts such as these fill the soul with wonder, and fix our reverence upon a solid foundation.

Here arises another speculation, infinitely interesting, the tracing the connection between the two great mysteries—that of the Eucharist and the Incarnation. 'It was love that prompted our Lord to seek by the Incarnation to contract a most intimate alliance with man by becoming man. But here He becomes united with the body and soul of one man only; and He provided the Eucharistic Sacrament to unite Himself with all, and thus engage all by this double union to love Him the more.' Various of the Fathers have thus considered the Eucharist a sort of 'extension of the Incarnation'.

'Now, what is the secret,' asks Faber, 'of this undying energy' (of the Incarnation) 'which crosses over ages of time and continents of earth, and waxes no weaker by distance and duration? It must be looked for in that perpetual presence within His Church which our Lord promised in the Gospel, in His Blessed Sacrament itself. *Nothing will explain the phenomena of the Church except the Blessed Sacrament.*'

A thought connected with the Holy Eucharist—and it is the same with the Passion—is its undivided efficacy and relation to each individual, as though there were no one else besides in the wide world to share the benefit. Salvation, with its attendant works and operation, is laid out on this scheme, and is furnished and provided for one single soul. And that soul is so vast and so expanded, that it spreads over the entire firmament and fills the world itself. So do we take a tiny leaf in our hand, and the microscope shows it to be a mass of minute living things, uncountable; while below is yet another domain of life, quite as boundless, and beyond the ken of microscopes.

There is a fine expression of St. Gregory Nazianzen, which furnishes a glimmering of this great truth: 'Man upon earth,' he says, 'is like an inversion of a great temple, *in the little temple of the universe*'; that is, the soul with its aspirations and ultimate destiny is actually *larger* than all the world together. Our low earthly eyes measure everything by the low earthly standards we are accustomed to. We fancy everything must be according to the scale of earth and earthy. It is thus that a clever artist used to contend that, even in art, there was no such thing as greatness or smallness, and that some tiny exquisitely engraved Roman gem, showing some face full of suggestion, soul, and expression, was actually as *large*, to all intents and purposes, as a huge canvas. We are always inclined to believe that *reality* must be associated with matter, and that thought and the spiritual world here and hereafter have something unreal or vapoury. Yet even in our earthly dispensation it will be found, without resorting to metaphysical reasoning, that nearly the whole of the material order and its presumed realities—the enjoyments, feelings, &c.—all virtually depend on thoughts and associations, and are indeed furnished by ourselves and our imagination. One day, it may be, we shall see that chemistry amounts to little more than that one portion of matter or dirt is connected with another, or is mixed with it; but where *all is dirt*, such minutiæ lose interest. Neither, in this world, is there anything large or small, or black or white, or bitter or sweet, or long or short—but all these things are relative. A painter can make a dark grey appear staring white by surrounding it with dark colours. An hour is long to a person in pain, but flies like minutes to one enjoying himself. A short man is a giant to smaller animals.

This idea of the Eucharist being exclusively, as it were, for one, and yet for all, is explained by Alger, who furnishes this happy illustration. 'It is,' he says, 'as with a speaker who is addressing a large audience, and where each individual hears every word as if it were addressed only to himself. And though the speaker utters his words only once, they are multiplied for everyone in the assembly; and though to each is communicated the whole speech, he deprives no one else of a single word.'

Again. There is a mysterious, wonderful connection between the fall of our first parents and the great compensation or restoration furnished to us by our Lord. They were allowed to partake of everything in the garden, but were forbidden to touch the Tree of Life. By a bountiful reversal we are invited to refrain from the other tempting fruits in the garden of the world, and commanded to eat of the great Tree of Life. And here the same spirit of contrariety reigns; for in both cases all seem to hanker after what is forbidden, and to avoid doing what is so solemnly enjoined. 'The devil,' says the Abbot Rupert, 'tempted our first parents. "Eat this fruit," he said, "and you shall be as gods." They believed him, though God Himself had warned them that death would be their portion the moment they ate of it. To supply a remedy for this disorder our Saviour now tempts us in His turn, saying, "Eat of My Body and drink of My Blood, and you shall be as gods". In this truly divine fashion, and in almost the same form, is the original fall repaired, "*You shall be as gods*". In the case of ordinary eating we change food into our own substance, but here we are changed into this heavenly food. As Job exclaimed, "How can one eat what is insipid and what is not preserved with salt ; or can any man taste that which bringeth death ? " '

It is easy to see what an extraordinary influence on the events of the world this supernatural presence must have had, during the nearly nineteen hundred years which have elapsed since its institution. It is, indeed, the main element of resistance, the source of strength in the long, perpetual struggle always going on between the powers of good and evil. The banners of the just have always been kept flying through the aid of millions of Masses said daily—through millions of communions and attendant prayers and aspirations. This power, from its ubiquity and universality, must be reckoned with by the forces of the world ; it confronts them at every point. Indeed, it is enough to state that, when there is this actual presence of our Lord upon earth, there can be no defeat. All history, therefore, which leaves this supernatural factor out, is but a maimed, imperfect record.*

For the Catholic the results of this Sacrament, in the way of furnishing strength, &c., are little short of miraculous in their power and certainty. We are often apt to forget our Saviour's assurance not only that He will come to live in us, but that we shall live in Him ; that our nature is to be changed into His. 'Whence comes,' asks St. Lawrence, 'that power we see in body and soul? Whence that renewal of the interior man, that fervour of charity, that sweetness and gentleness, abundance of peace, longing to advance in virtue? By the devout participation in this Sacrament, enmities cease, quarrels end, vice becomes distaste-

* F. Bridgett, in his profound work *The History of the Holy Eucharist*, in the chapter entitled ' The Key-Stone,' has expounded the same view.

ful, we love purity and despise things of earth. A man becomes a changed being. He curbs his tongue, loves silence, cultivates prayer, maintains brotherly love, practises purity of heart, and everything that is acceptable to God. All which is owing to the amiable presence of our Lord.' This is, indeed, but natural; for, as Father Vaubert says, once we hold the image of our Saviour within us, it follows, as of course, that we must copy Him. 'A cutting from a good tree,' says St. Thomas, 'when it is grafted on another, imparts its peculiar virtues, takes away its unwholesome juices, and causes it to bear fruit like its own.' Indeed, as Bossuet puts it, 'Once our Saviour has given Himself to us, *we must expect no peace* if we wish to keep Him'.

IV.

Of Spiritual Dryness.

This great Sacrament is figured in the manna which was given to the Israelites. But there is a passage in the Book of Wisdom which applies with wonderful particularity. 'Thou hast given to Thy people the food of angels. Without need of working! for it this bread has come down from heaven ready prepared, and is stored with all the most delicious savours. This nourishment was a testimony of Thy bounty to Thy children.' It adapted itself to their inclination, and according as their appetite changed so it changed its savour. 'Thus the Sacrament,' says St. Cyprian, 'adapts itself to all tastes, and by its marvellous virtue makes each one feel, according to the measure of his preparation, the pleasure which he desires.' But it is not given to all to enjoy these interior delights. In some cases it is owing to temperament and special circumstances, and St. Thomas uses some happy images to express this difference. There are two fashions of enjoyment, he says, in the natural order—one based on the common pleasure of the senses, the other of an intellectual sort. Thus the miser, though he has none from the spending of his hoard, still enjoys the very thought of having it in his coffers. The sick man, though his medicines are distasteful, relishes them because they are helping him back to health. The Eucharist, says F. Vaubert, can give one or other of these satisfactions. For the true and faithful soul the mere thought that he is receiving a treasure which comprises the whole riches of heaven, the real Physician of souls and the key of all the virtues, is in itself an ennobling pleasure without any of the interior enjoyment.

The very habit and routine of pious practices pursued through a long course sometimes brings with it this sort of *tiédeur*, which seems to enfeeble the springs of action. Bishop Butler, in his wonderful argument, *The Analogy*, which offers many truly Catholic lights, has, in his own convincing way, accounted for this failure of emotional feeling by the difference that exists between what he calls 'active' and 'passive' habits. These can scarcely coexist, and are destructive of each other. Thus the being moved or suffering at the spectacle of poverty, grief, wounds, sickness, &c., is a proper incentive to action, that is, to relieve such suffering; but in practice it is found that the habit of indulging in such emotions, unsupported by action, will actually destroy all inclination to the latter.

It is the same with people who weep over novels and plays, or expend their affections on animals. On the other hand, persons engaged in *actions* of benevolence and charity, such as doctors and nurses, will find the sentimental feeling of compassion evaporate with action, while the *active* principle becomes a habit and stronger every day. There is a class of really 'good' persons, 'slaves of duty,' as they are called, who are often found disagreeable because they seem to have got rid of all feeling, and have made their nerves, as Mrs. Siddons said, 'like cart ropes'. For the same reason we often find people with 'beautiful ideas of religion' eager about 'functions,' church decorations, and rosaries, ever engrossed in the recitation of long, set prayers, but altogether failing in *acts*. A modern poet expresses this exactly :

> 'Prune thou thy words, the thoughts control
>   That o'er thee swell and throng;
> They will condense within thy soul,
>   And change to purpose strong:
> But he who lets his feelings run
>   In soft luxurious flow,
> Shrinks when hard service must be done,
>   And faints at every woe.
> Faith's meanest deed more favour bears,
>   Where hearts and wills are weighed,
> Than brightest transports, choicest prayers,
>   Which bloom their hour and fade.'

But the passage in *The Analogy* is so forcible, so conclusive and instructive, that we shall do a service to the thoughtful and practical-minded by furnishing the very words :

'As habits belonging to the body are produced by external acts, so habits of the mind are matured by the exertion of inward practical principles—*i.e.*, *by carrying them into act*. But going over the theory of virtue in one's thoughts, talking well and drawing the picture of it,—this is so far from forming a habit of it in him who thus employs himself, *that it may harden the mind in a contrary course*, and form a habit of insensibility to all moral considerations.' And mark the reason. 'For passive impressions by being repeated grow weaker. Thoughts by often passing through the mind are felt less sensibly; being accustomed to danger begets intrepidity, *i.e.*, lessens fear; to distress, lessens pity. And from these two observations it must follow that active habits may be forming by a course of acting upon such motives, while these motives are growing less sensible.'

This valuable analysis will be found to explain many things. It applies to bad as well as to good habits. Thus repeated acts of a venial or of a more serious kind will gradually enfeeble the opposing good principle, until the evil practice becomes a habit. Many persons are fond of multiplied or accumulated prayers, abundant decades, offices, &c., excellent practices, no doubt, but needing to be vivified, as it were, by a principle. The result is often a habit of purely mechanical prayer. The person comes at last to be engrossed with the task of getting successfully through all his labours, but often with the result that the spiritual principle—that of prayer—evaporates, and gives place to words; much as the Chinese have a 'praying machine' inscribed with efficacious prayers, each turn of which is equivalent to a recitation.

It will be easy to apply this principle to the case of the habit of communion, where it might be expected that familiarity would enfeeble a devout appreciation. But here come in the gifts of grace and other blessings which, in the case of the truly pious, only increase with time. The ordinary communicant whose standard of perfection is not so high will find Butler's principle operate; with repetition the emotion will weaken, but, on the other hand, a habit, and the incidents of habit—the general habit of communion—though coldly performed, becomes, at the least, a barrier against sin; sinlessness itself becomes a habit, as the tendency to sin, through lack of use, wears out. There is a habit of watchfulness—there is at least a sense of shame—which prevents us yielding, save under great pressure, to even the most venial sins. Thus, at least, is secured 'the beginning of wisdom,' which, if not of a very high type, is of a practical, wholesome kind, and offers a basis for future efforts.

There is another train of speculation nearly connected with this. It is when we think over seriously the nature of what is called *an act* that we find out what should be the character of true piety and of true prayer. We are apt to associate this term of 'act' with something *physical;* but an act of thought is just as real. A sinful act of thought shows us at once what should be the nature of a *good* act of thought, viz., that we are ready on the instant to follow it up by some physical act. Even in law it has always been held that the physical part is, on the whole, immaterial; for it is the *intention* that makes the act. It is seldom, indeed, that we think of the final and irrevocable character of all genuine 'acts,' whether in the material or immaterial world. There is a perfect analogy between both. A tree is cut down, an egg-shell is broken; but not all the wit of man, nor his science and power—neither the king, nor the king's men, can undo or repair it. There can be piecing or glueing or restoration: but the severance is eternal. It may be so with an immaterial, sinful, or righteous action: it is *done:* it cannot be repaired.

Earnest good will and purpose in avoiding trifling faults begets habit: a habit in trifles leads curiously up to the magnifying their importance, much as in practising a musical instrument perfection in some small exercise secures much greater results. But let us hear on this point the wise and quaint old Chaucer, not commonly credited with much gift of preaching.

In his 'Parson's Tale' he gives us some admirable directions as to venial and other sins. 'If he be very penitent, he shall first bewail the sins that he hath done, and steadfastly purpose in his heart to have shrift of mouth, and to do satisfaction, and never to do things for which he ought more to bewail. Or else his repentance may not avail. For, as saith St. Isidor, *he is a japer and a gaber*, and no very repentant, that soon again doth things for which he hath repented. Weeping, and not for to stint to sin, may not avail.' Better still what follows: 'Soothly, when man loveth any creature more than Jesus Christ our Creator, his is deadly sin; and venial sin is it if man loveth Jesus Christ less than him; and, therefore, if a man charge himself with many such venial sins, but, if so be that he some time discharge him of them by shrift, they must fall lightly, *amenuse* (destroy) in him all the love he hath to Jesus Christ, and in this wise *skippeth venial sin* into deadly sin. And hearken this example: a great wave of the sea cometh some time with so great violence that it drencheth the ship; and the same harm doth some time the small drops of water that enter through a little crevice into the hold, if men be so negligent that they discharge them not by time.'

In that gracious book *The Devout Life*, St. Francis de Sales dwells on the contrast between what may be called the sentimental and more practical forms of piety, illustrating it, as his wont is, with many picturesque images. 'I would say, then, that devotion does not consist in that sweetness, consolation, and visible tenderness which provoke tears and sighs, and gives us a certain agreeable savour and satisfaction in our spiritual exercises. No, this is not the same thing as devotion; for there are many souls which experience these enjoyments and consolations, and nevertheless are vicious, and, consequently, have no true love of God, much less any true devotion. . . . So there are some persons who, when they reflect on the goodness of God and the Passion of Christ, are powerfully moved to sighs, tears, prayers, and other devout actions, whence you might suppose that their hearts were seized with a very fervent devotion; but when they are proved, we find, that as the passing rains of a hot summer, though they fall heavily on the earth, do not penetrate it, and only bring forth mushrooms, even so these tears and emotions in a corrupt heart do not penetrate it, and are altogether fruitless.

'And assuredly the smallest religious consolation we receive is in every way superior to the most delectable worldly joys. And just as those who chew the herb *Cytisus* are so satisfied with its sweetness that they feel neither hunger nor thirst, so those to whom God has given the celestial manna of His inward sweetness and consolations, cannot seek or receive those of the world, or, at all events, cannot take delight or rest their affections in them. Such heavenly consolations are as foretastes of the eternity of bliss which God gives to those souls who seek it; they resemble the sugared bribes we give to children; they are as cordial waters given by God to comfort the soul, and sometimes they are the pledges of everlasting rewards.'

But, as Bourdaloue asks: 'Is it credible that a soul could have a repugnance for this heavenly sustenance, which is God Himself, or could we ever convince ourselves that a bread which is capable of being the food of angels should be found insipid by men, or that they should find it a pain to use it? . . . The most fatal sign of failing health is a repulsion to healthy food. To lose our taste for communion is one of the most alarming signs in our condition, and not to be disturbed at finding this repulsion, and at living on in this state with indifference, or without anxiety, is the final stage of being hardened, and the sure proof of a disordered conscience, and of one, it may be, in peril of being lost.' So, all labour, save that of prayer, will fail: the remedy is to ask or pray that one may be 'drawn' by Him, to whom no one can come unless 'drawn'. And the aid of our Blessed Lady should be invoked, her connection with this Sacrament being of the closest kind. 'The Word,' says St. Augustine, forcibly, 'formed itself a Body from the pure flesh of Mary, His Mother: in this flesh He lived while on earth, and this same flesh He gives us to eat now.'

Father de Ravignan has explained this very clearly. No one, after reading what he tells us, can say that he has not the remedy in his own hands. 'If this relish for pious things be wanting, many other things will be wanting; for what is done without interest or taste is done badly, or, at least, is painful, and courage often is wanting to carry it through. In such cases we find that we drag ourselves, rather than fly, to prayer, meditation, and even to the communion. By an unfortunate delusion it is fancied that to obtain this feeling of unction and fervour of piety, so precious in our dealings with God, it is sufficient to rely on our own proper efforts. The result is that we fatigue and worry ourselves and grow discontented; so that we miss the point, which is, that devotion is a gift of God and of the Holy Spirit. It belongs to Him alone to give us this *gout* for divine things. He may try us with pains and sufferings, but will make us discover this heavenly need of the soul, which, no matter what its state, will find out the necessity of being restored to God. . . . So have no fear. Ask and you shall receive. Do not be discouraged, for Jesus has promised us His aid and His love.' In other words, all is the result of favour and grace, and we have the sure, unerring words of our Saviour that no man can come to Him unless He 'draw him'.

The old-established sinner, who, for his whole life almost, has been lost to grace, deludes himself that an unsurmountable barrier has shut him off from the reformation he desires, simply because he has no *emotional* feeling of sorrow, and has perhaps a strong affection for his sins. How often has this declaration been heard: 'It is of no use; I feel nothing . . . my heart is stony; it is too late'. He looks for a special gift of sorrow, to be obtained by prayer; but to pray with earnestness and sincerity seems itself to require a gift or grace; and so from this lamentable state, comes an apparent 'dead-lock,' and extrication seems impossible. Our great poet-philosopher has described this state of mind in the instance of the King in his *Hamlet:*

> 'What then? what rests?
> Try what repentance can: What can it not?
> Yet what can it, when one can not repent?
> O wretched state! O bosom, black as death!
> O limèd soul; that struggling to be free,
> Art more engag'd! Help, angels, make assay!
> Bow, stubborn knees! and, heart, with strings of steel,
> Be soft as sinews of the new-born babe;
> All may be well!'

This condition represents vividly the state of many a 'limèd soul'. But this almost inspired writer, it will be seen, reached to the true remedy, viz., 'Bow, stubborn knees'. He knew, too, that a favourable result would follow, and that 'all may be well'.

Once on a time, one of these habitual sinners related to me his curious history. He was a man of the world, but with a resolute, 'business-like' mind. Some serious reflections as to his state had of late occurred to him. There was no possibility of his life amending; the years went by like fruit-laden ships, and he was only likely to become more firmly fixed in his course. The last hour would suddenly arrive and surprise him in this state. All this he forecasted and pondered over. This sort of fatalist progress, leading him slowly and surely to destruction, without chance of release, often struck him with terror. But what was he to do? The old 'stock' objection always barred his way—he felt neither sorrow nor regret; nor could he, by reading pious works, excite it. The wells were dried up. How illusory, he thought, too, with bitterness, were those assurances he heard from pulpits, that all one had to do to be saved was to repent. Being of a practical turn, he said at last one day to himself: 'These are divine assurances. Let me bring all this to a point. One cannot do more than one can. Yet here am I, willing to do what is necessary.'

In this state he repaired one night to a church where an eminent preacher was giving a mission. By some wonderful interposition or miracle, the words from the pulpit seemed to be pointed directly to him and to his case. After describing, as my hearer said, a sinner, habitual and hardened, the preacher admitted that he could conceive such shrinking away and drawing back, from a sense that he was beyond repentance and felt no sorrow. Then, taking a calm, business-like tone, he bade such earnestly strike, and no longer wait till this sort of feeling arrived. 'Go at once,' he cried; 'go to the confessional; present yourself with good, set purpose. Do, act, *and do and act at once.* Stand not idly waiting for sorrow. *Action* is the best form of sorrow. Tell your sins, and *then* you will see!' Amazed and bewildered at this advice which so exactly met his difficulties, the prodigal went next day to a clergyman, and told him his whole state. With a quiet air of business the other at once led the way to the church. 'But I am not ready, not prepared, I must have time,' protested the other. 'Never mind,' was the reply, 'begin at once.' In a halting, confused way, the penitent did as he was directed, and with the most wonderful result. Instantly what he had sought for so long came: the rock was softened, his past life lay open, he felt a new man, was confounded at the almost miraculous change that had been wrought in him in a moment, and which endures to this hour.

Thus it is that these words, 'Ask and you shall receive,' furnish the Christian with a magic talisman, with which he can work prodigies. And what plea can anyone urge, when at the last grand process he has to own that he has persistently and stupidly neglected to use this infallible instrument, available in every difficulty? The words of our Lord are eternal, and eternally true. They are eternal acts, which cannot be undone. Whatever the difficulty, there is the remedy at hand. Are you indifferent, hardened, ask for light and warmth: are you troubled and in suffering, ask for strength and indifference. Even if the result does not *appear* to answer, you may wait, and can urge the justification of having done what was enjoined.

In a charming passage, St. Francis of Sales dwells on the same idea:

'Let everything be overcast and overturned, not only around us, but within us: that is to say, let our soul be sad or joyful, in sweetness or bitterness, in peace or in trouble, in darkness or in light, in temptation or in repose, in satisfaction or disgust, in dryness or consolation, burnt with the sun or refreshed with the dew: however it be, still the needle of the heart must earnestly tend to the love of God its Saviour. Tribulation nor distress, nor death nor life, nor present sorrow nor fear of things to come, nor the devices of evil spirits, nor the height of consolation, nor the depth of affliction, nor softness nor dryness, nothing shall separate us from that holy charity which is rooted and built up in Jesus Christ.

'This absolute resolution never to forsake God or leave His tender love serves to balance our souls and preserve them in holy evenness, amidst the unevenness of this life's restless motion, just as bees, when they are carried about with the wind, embrace stones in order that they may keep their balance, and not be so at the mercy of the storm.'

'It is a delightful thing,' wrote the truly pious Gordon, 'to be a fatalist . . . to accept that, when things happen, and not before, God has for some wise reason so ordained them. All things, not only the great things, but all the circumstances of life—that is what to me is meant by the words "Ye are dead". We have nothing further to do when the scroll of events is unrolled than to accept them as being for the best; but before it is unrolled, it is another matter; for you would not say, "I sat still, and let things happen". With this belief, all I can say is that, amidst troubles and worries, no one can have peace till he thus stays upon his God; that gives a superhuman strength.'

In short, purpose, perseverance, steadiness, independence of all gusts and humours, and the going forward steadily in the one course, without looking to the right or to the left—here is the talisman. Cardinal Newman touches this profoundly in one of his early hymns:

' Once, as I brooded o'er my guilty state,
A fever seized me, duties to devise,
To buy me interest in my Saviour's eyes ;
Not that His love I would extenuate,
But scourge and penance, masterful self-hate!
Or gift of cost, served by an artifice
To quell my restless thoughts, and envious sighs
And doubts, which fain heaven's peace would antedate.
Thus as I tossed, He said, " E'en holiest deeds
Shroud not the soul from God, nor soothe its needs:
Deny thee thine own fears, and wait the end ".
  Stern lesson!'

'Those who keep far from Thee shall perish,' says St. Chrysostom—a warning which applies particularly to that large class, as it may be feared, of well-meaning, 'easy-going' Catholics, who live in much esteem and respectability, who 'eat and drink the Body of the Lord,' but rarely, by way of qualification for membership of the Church, rather than for their support and nutriment.

We may not, of course, judge these cases harshly. Many are, no doubt, so pressed with heavy duties and contending distractions, that they have not time for this religious duty. But experience of the carelessness of human character makes it probable that here there is also little taste or eagerness to approach. By analogy in the ordinary life, when a course of restorative diet and treatment is prescribed, the chief element of recovery is that the system be pursued steadily, and without break; for the object is to renew the strength and substitute a strong system for the old one. This can only be secured by repeated and regular administration, and is the 'business-like' view which the worldling, as he may be called, should take of his spiritual state, recognising the truth that this divine nutriment is the basis of life and health.

'I am the living bread, which came down from heaven: if any man eat of this bread, he shall live for ever: and the bread that I will give is My flesh for the life of the world. The Jews therefore strove among themselves, saying: How can this man give us His flesh to eat? Then Jesus said to them: Amen, amen, I say unto you, except you eat the flesh of the Son of Man, and drink His blood, you shall not have life in you. He that eateth My flesh, and drinketh My blood, hath everlasting life: and will raise him up in the last day. For My flesh is meat indeed: and My blood is drink indeed.'

It thus becomes a serious reflection for the man

of the world, that this having 'life in us' is virtually *compulsory;* for it is not only declared to be the only method of obtaining the 'life,' but, unless the attempt be made properly, thoroughly, and in a worthy way to secure success, a terrible penalty is menaced. 'For he that eateth and drinketh unworthily, eateth and drinketh judgment to himself.' So that our worldling stands between these two perilous alternatives: if he abstain he perishes of inanition, and forfeits his chance of salvation; and if he approach unprepared, he is lost. He must, however, face both issues.

It is remarkable, indeed, as St. Chrysostom points out, that our Saviour never mentions the Holy Eucharist without promising to give us 'life' along with it. 'Never forget,' exclaims St. Bernard, 'that the first man, in his fall, drew us all down with him. We have fallen on a heap of stones and in the mud: and thus have not been merely stained and dirtied all over, but have been cruelly bruised and cut. We may be cleansed in due time: but this is not so with our lusts, which take vast trouble and much dressing to heal. Baptism washes us, and thus annuls our condemnation. But then is left the imperious cravings of the flesh, and cupidity; and what is to cure this greed—this open sore?' Then he adds: 'but you have the remedy—the Body and Blood of the Saviour, which has two certain results. It diminishes all tendency to the smallest sins, and prevents us yielding to great ones. So that if you feel no longer those violent tumults of anger, envy, &c., remember to give thanks to Jesus Christ, for it is the virtue of His Sacrament that was worked in you.'

'We ought,' says P. Lallemand, 'to desire neither to see nor admire anything else on earth save the Holy Sacrament. Were God Himself capable of admiring, He would admire nothing but this mystery and that of the Incarnation. As for us, what is it we admire? Honour, human talents, other vile and despicable trifles, which one day will fill us with confusion when at the hour of death we shall see how we have treated our Lord in the Holy Sacrament.' This is, in fact, but the Spirit of Truth, 'whom the world cannot receive'. 'Terrible words,' says the author of *Reflections and Prayers*. 'If I have the spirit of the world, I cannot then receive the Spirit of Jesus Christ. Our Lord does not say that the world *will* not receive the Spirit of Truth, but that it *cannot*—it is absolutely unable to do so.'

There is, in truth, a logic so pitiless in these things, that we find ourselves obliged to veil the true state of things from our own eyes by all sorts of devices. *You cannot serve God and mammon.* There is the immutable truth. If your very eye scandalise you, you are to pluck it out. Yet we are all striving to compound, as it were; and, if we were put on our oath, would have to own that mammon has far the more service. As St. Chrysostom says: '*There is but the one sorrow in the world*—to be deprived of this heavenly bread'; and such in the early ages was the accepted feeling of the congregations, who, when they were interdicted for a short time as a punishment, fell into a profound melancholy and shed torrents of tears. With these may be contrasted modern worlding absentees. 'With what tranquillity do they not bear this separation! With what indolence do they not see themselves withdrawn from the God of their salvation! With what insensibility do they grow accustomed not merely to feel no affliction, but even to find themselves comfortable! The truth is, that commonly the pious life is found a heavy burden: it troubles or interrupts their foolish pleasures, which to enjoy without interruption or trouble they at length give up altogether. To communicate they have to be watchful and constrain themselves. It is more convenient to stay away altogether.'

The same thought Bourdaloue has enforced in his own trenchant style.

'The great maxim which is to regulate the sinner's conduct as to communion turns on the never separating these two inviolable truths: first, that Jesus Christ *commands* us to eat His flesh; the second, that He *forbids* us to eat unworthily. The flesh of the Man-God is meant for the food of our soul, though this very food may become a poison for him who eats in a state of sin.'

'Now if the sinner,' he goes on, 'keeps hold of these two truths, without separating them, he is in the right road of return to God. If he separate them he is lost. This must be his reasoning: Jesus Christ forbids me to eat His flesh so long as I am in sin. On the other hand, I shall not have life unless I eat. I must, therefore, get out of my present state to become capable of eating. I cannot be disposed for obeying both one and the other of these commandments—the first for Christ's interest, the second for my own. There is, therefore, only one issue, viz., a change of life.'

How true and compelling is this logic! But the dilemma is complete, and, as the Preacher says, there is but the one issue. He goes on: 'Fear, as St. Francis de Sales says, to approach this Holy Table, and fear not to approach it. Fear to approach if you have not on the wedding garment, that is, grace; and fear not to approach, for it is only God's enemies who are excluded from it. The food offered to you is death-giving for you, if you do not make a proper discerning through the spirit of faith; but it is also a health-giving meat, without which the Son of God will not remain in you nor you in Him. So tremble as you take this meat: but tremble even more if you do not take it for the excuse that you are not prepared.'

'I see among you,' once said St. Augustine, 'some keeping away from communion because they feel guilty. But I tell such that if they remain in that condition, they only increase the weight and number of their sins by adding to them a fresh one, thus depriving themselves of the most necessary sovereign remedy. I conjure you, then, if anyone of you deem himself unworthy of communion, let him strive to make himself worthy; for whoever is not worthy of this Sacrament is not worthy of God.' He, therefore, would 'exhort and persuade' all to approach every Sunday.

This thought is beautifully expressed by Keble in one of his hymns:

> 'O agony of wavering thought!
> When sinners first so near are brought,
> It is my Maker—dare I stay?
> My Saviour—dare I turn away?'

But there is a passage in one of Bourdaloue's discourses so searching, so profound in its analysis, and so profitable, that I am convinced that everyone who reads it through will be grateful to me for giving it here. Mark well, 'perpend, and inwardly digest,' I would say, and, at the same time, admire the wisdom which seems to have filled these great French divines.

How is it, he asks, that worldly occupations should cause this repugnance, unless from the relaxation into which they cause us to fall? 'In this round of dissipations we easily forget God and all that is connected with Him. We are only attentive to what is going on in the world. The heart devoted to one object grows indifferent to all others; we lose little by little those good dispositions for pious duties; we grow less and less inclined to the Christian duties; we have only a languishing faith and uncertain hope, a poor and sluggish charity; and then sets in that repugnance to communion and the making of it a burden.

'For here is what happens. We retain sufficient religion to wish not to communicate unworthily, and our eyes are sufficiently opened to see that the communion scarcely accords with the relaxed life that we live. But we love our easy and enjoyable life. All that interferes with it seems insupportable. Hence the idea of communion becomes irksome. We say what the Jews said of the manna: Our soul nauseates this food.' The Preacher then draws a picture of what follows: 'So soon as a soul instead of feeling itself drawn to the Holy Table finds itself in exactly the opposite disposition; when it has become a pain, a subject of struggle, it is certain that it will strive to communicate as seldom as possible, that it will always be finding excuses to abstain. And with what result? The fewer communions the fewer graces; the less struggle the less vigilance or zeal for advancing. In consequence of the fewer communions the more relaxation and forgetfulness of God. *Mark well what I say.* The less communion, less there is of grace. And why? Because we keep further away from Jesus Christ, the

Source of all graces, and who nowhere confers them with such abundance as in His own Sacrament. The less that we communicate the less strength we have, communion being the only bread of life. The less we communicate the less watchfulness over self, the less zeal for perfection and advancement. Because there is no longer the effectual curb to check us, the most active spirit to rouse us, the most pressing of reasons to excite us—and this is the prospect of an impending communion. We are not immediately bound to repress our passions, to elevate every action, weigh our words, and thus remain in a continued state of preparation; and finally, because we are no longer touched by those secret impulses, interior reproaches, divine lights, and communications from God, which are the fruits of communion. And so the heart grows colder and colder day by day. God withdraws, and the world takes His place.'

This eloquent passage carries conviction with it, and is supported by experience. So might we follow the sure and slow stages of a disease, the progress of a taste for drink, and other vices. Happily the Preacher supplied the remedy, in whose power he is as confident as in that of the disease.

'It is,' he says, 'to understand thoroughly the *principles* of this repugnance as well as its consequences. Reason with yourself on this practice. I see people approach the Holy Table much more frequently than I do; approaching, too, with ardent desires. I see that their life is more edifying than mine. There was a time, too, when I had the same ardour; and thus, too, *my* life was better than it is now. But how am I to stop this habitual torpor? How is it to end? What are its perils?

You must struggle against this repugnance. A sick person who turns away from meat, and who finds his strength failing him, exerts himself, and does all he can to force himself to take food. In proportion to his struggles, he gradually recovers strength. You have this repugnance; never mind, communicate; after all you will have the proper disposition. It may be a long contest; you will have to fight against the revolt in your own breast. But this will not be all in vain. God notices the wish you show to recover Him, and will let Himself incline towards you. He will allow the dews of heaven to descend upon you. He will overwhelm you with that benediction of sweetness which He has promised to His elect; and you will experience what a thousand others have experienced, and which it only rests with yourself to enjoy like them, that, having come to the Holy Table prompted by a pure faith and a sincere religion, though without any sensible affection or relish, you will pass from it filled with consolation. Finally, apply to God Himself with frequent, humble prayers. Ask Him to bend your heart, to draw you to Himself, and say to Him, with the spouse in the Canticle, *Draw me after Thee!*'

The good and imperfect, says St. Francis de Sales, should communicate frequently, the first to maintain their perfection, the second to become better; the strong lest they become weak, the weak that they become strong. Those at ease and with leisure, because they have leisure; the busy, because 'he who labours much and is loaded with pains ought to eat solid meats and that frequently'. What can be more sensible than this? And what a force in his expostulation: 'O Philothea, what reply shall reprobate Christians be able to make when the Just Judge shall upbraid them with their folly, or rather madness, in having involved themselves in eternal death, since it was so easy to have maintained themselves in life and health by feeding on His Body, which He has left them for that intention. *Miserable wretches! He will say, why did you die, having the food and fruit of life at your command?*'

Finally, he enforces frequent communion by this worthy image: 'Communicate thou frequently, then, Philothea, and believe me, as hares in our mountains become white in winter because they neither see nor eat anything but snow, so, by approaching to, and eating beauty, purity, and goodness itself, you will become altogether fair, pure, and virtuous'.

V.

The Eucharist figured in the New Testament.

We have thus seen how the great Sacrament is, as it were, intertwined with the whole spiritual order, and how it underlies the whole scheme of salvation. More wonderful is it to trace this strict connection in the utterances of our Lord Himself, who, as it were, furnishes to His disciple a whole treasury of thoughts and aspirations for the reception of His Sacrament. Not only does He thus give Himself, but He supplies fitting forms of love, gratitude, and desire; so that it may be said the communicant's best prayer-book is the Scripture itself.

In the Apocalypse there is a mysterious passage that seems to point at the Holy Eucharist: 'To him that overcometh I will give the hidden manna;

and I will give him *a white counter:* and in that counter a new name written which no man knoweth but he that receiveth it'. It will be noted what a remarkable, particular indication is found here, not of the fruit merely, but of the form of the Sacrament, as also of the conditions of receiving it fittingly. In Isaiah, too (iv. 6), there is a prophecy which seems to allude to the same :

'The Lord,' said Isaias, 'will create on Mount Sion, in the place where He shall have been invoked, a dark cloud by day and a bright flame by night ; His tabernacle shall be, for those who love it, a shade against the heat of the day, a place of security, a hidden retreat against the tempest and the rain during the night'.

St. Augustine tells us, in a passage quoted by Massillon, that there is another important use of the miracles of our Lord besides the proofs of their credibility and their value as evidence of His sacred mission—'The faithful should study them in view of being enlightened and instructed, and search into the very depths of the divine traits they exhibit and which are so fruitful as guides for life and religion. All these miracles have a language of their own, and it is only lax and carnal followers that see in them riddles and hyperboles.'

Massillon points out how the miracle of the multiplication of the loaves is particularly significant of the Holy Eucharist, and how in all the proceedings of the multitude before it took place ' may be noted the dispositions which should fit us for a worthy communion, while in all that followed we find signs of the fruits we should gather from the Sacrament'. It is interesting to follow the great preacher in this analysis, which might naturally escape many. Thus it will be seen that our Lord began by *curing* such of them as were afflicted with any maladies. He next proceeded to *instruct* them in many things, speaking to them of the kingdom of God. More remarkable still, He did not find them nourishment *at once;* He waited 'till the day was well spent,' and the hour for the repast gone by, when hunger began to be felt. He then made all sit down upon the grass. ' Here we have,' says the preacher, ' literally all the proper dispositions which should be entertained for communion.'

For, first, we must be 'cured' before partaking of the bread of heaven. The cure must be solid and permanent, 'fixing those everlasting vicissitudes of the heart'. Not that we must assume that relapses after communion prove that there has been no cure. 'For, alas! what is man but a weak traveller in a strange land, who is never secure against surprises or open attacks; an unhappy creature, who carries in his heart the source of all his evils and the weapons of his own defeat. Should, however, on passing from the altar, you find yourself weak as before, as bitter against your neighbour, as worldly in your tastes and habits, is not this a certain token that you have come with death in your bosom, and the shameful sore of sin in your soul? The truth is, cures by grace are not cures of a day. And as grace only succeeds by a slow and imperceptible progress, so it only departs gradually and by slow and imperceptible degrees.'

Our Lord also desired, before giving that nourishment, that the people should *feel* hunger. It was then, remarks St. Augustine, that His mercy selected the moment to feed them. For 'the Flesh of Jesus Christ has this special quality, it will nourish only when it is relished'. Massillon then describes the nature of this relish: '"Tis to find a thousand times more dainties at the table of the Lord than in the honey and in the tents of sinners; to desire it with ardour, await it anxiously, and count no day in life so happy as that on which we are permitted to draw near: 'tis to find in it the single comfort of our exile, the softening of our pains, peace in our troubles, strength in our temptations, recovery in our languor, light in our difficulties; it is to fall, like the prophet, into dryness'.

'You cannot,' says the author of *The Devout Life* very forcibly, 'consider our Saviour in an action more full of love, or more tender than this, in which He changes Himself into meat, that so He may penetrate our souls, and unite Himself most intimately to the heart and to the body of His faithful.'

Then as to the results of the miracle. 'All the great multitude "was filled"—that is, "satiated".— and the quantity left was so great that the fragments had to be collected, and our Lord directed that they should be taken care of "lest they be lost". Finally, the people were so struck with the prodigy, so satisfied with the nourishment furnished to them, that they wished to make their Benefactor king. Here at once are exhibited all the fruits we ought to gain from communion.' The following out these analogies is singularly interesting in itself, and adds to the richness of the Sacrament by carrying on the continuity of our Lord's presence and renewing and repeating His life in our own day.

The same application to the Sacrament is found in all the other episodes, and is even more particularly shown in the account of Zaccheus, whose behaviour to our Lord and reception at our Lord's hands offer a pattern and encouragement for all. Nor is there anything forced in this similitude; Zaccheus showed all the dispositions of a worthy communicant. Our Lord received him exactly as though His Sacrament were then existing, with the words, 'This day salvation has come to this house'. Here we find again all the stages of a good communion. The penitent first 'proving' himself by making the eager exertion to climb up into a sycamore tree in his longing to see the Saviour: the instant reward of his exertion: 'Come down; this day I must abide in thy house': followed by the receiving him with joy: the making of atonement and doing good: and the final encouraging assurance and recognition: 'This day salvation has come to thy house'.

He then, we are told, 'stood before the Lord,' that is, waited patiently to receive his holy inspirations, which presently bore its fruits displayed in a complete change of heart and conversion. Then, half of his goods he gave to the poor, and he restored fourfold to those he had wronged: an example of charity and self-sacrifice.

Interesting also is the behaviour and reception of the many persons who approached our Lord asking for relief—all encouraging, as examples. Thus Bourdaloue points out that the woman who was so grievously sick, and so eager to come to him, said within herself: 'If I can only touch His robe, I shall be healed'. 'Note,' he says, 'that she did not think it necessary even to *tell* Him her case, or even to address Him a single word, and her faith was justified.'

The cases of the centurion and publican have also a 'note' of their own, and this application is more frequently made, as F. Bridgett has pointed out to me.

'St. Augustine has a profound remark as to these two men. One, the publican, received our Lord into his house with great joy. The other, the captain, bade our Lord *not* come to him, since he was not worthy of such a favour. St. Augustine remarks that these are different, and apparently contradictory, ways of showing reverence and devotion, but that these two *men did not quarrel with each other* as to which was right, and our Lord praised both. So, says St. Augustine, some show their love by frequent communion, others their reverence by less frequent. Either of these forms our Lord will accept. The only thing He will not accept is contempt or indifference.'

The parable of the prodigal has always been the favourite encouragement for the sinner, and seems to suit every condition of penitence. We know how he said to himself that he 'would arise and go to his father,' and how the latter, 'when he was yet a great way off, saw him, and ran and fell on his neck and kissed him'. He thus even anticipated the acknowledgment of sin and appeal for forgiveness. Then followed a formal act of confession and contrition : 'Father, I have sinned before heaven and before thee, and am no more worthy to be called thy son'. He was not only forgiven, but instantly forgiven ; for they were told to 'bring *quickly*' the best robe and the ring. The good Christian—who from long habit has brought his service of God to a sort of routine, holding sin of all degrees in horror—may have often repined to find his long devotions unrecognised, or unrequited with such affectionate transports. All seems reserved for sinners; and the worse the sinner, the more lovingly he is welcomed. This is often found in the natural order as well: as when the good servant, good husband, wife, or child are 'taken as a matter of course'. The answer to this is given in this striking parable. The exact objection was made. 'These many years have I served thee, and never have I broken thy commandments; *and yet thou hast never given me a kid that I might make merry with my friends.*' To whom came the answer and gentle rebuke: 'All that I have is thine'. In the Holy Communion the gift is so immense, so large, and yet so particular, that it is a gift to the individual, as much as if no other person in the world existed. And we are helped to the conception of this idea by the case of the boundless affection of a parent which is distributed to all her children, being *wholly* given to each, though multiplied. As St. Augustine says, 'God, in bestowing on men the gift of the Holy Eucharist, may be said to have exhausted the treasures of His divinity. By His almighty favour He can do whatever He pleases, can create a thousand worlds each more lovely than ours, but can never effect anything greater than the Holy Eucharist.' 'Jesus Christ,' says St. John Chrysostom, 'gives Himself to us with all that He possesses. He keeps back nothing.' How true, therefore, becomes the application of the words, 'All that I have is thine'.

Again, as we read carefully the history of Elias in the desert, we at every moment feel the likeness between the aid and comfort that was vouchsafed to him and what is given to us at the Holy Table. 'Elias exclaims, "Lord, it is enough, take now my soul"—a bitter complaint, common among souls weak in virtue, resounded unanswered in the desert. The Prophet, thinking himself abandoned, asked for death to relieve him from his sufferings. God sometimes feeds him by means of birds, which bring him bread and meat, common articles of food, which represent the first graces accorded to a sinner. At another time it is a poor widow who has only a handful of meal and a little oil remaining; this is a figure of the soul withered by the corrupting breath of the world, which has dried up the fountains of grace within her, and suffers her only to draw a feeble life even from Holy Communion. It is not until the moment when, completely separated from creatures, Elias abandons himself entirely to the direction of God, that heaven opens, "an angel descends," touches him, to arouse and restore his worn-out courage, and offers him a loaf of bread baked on the ashes. Mysterious image of the Holy Eucharist, which operates only in proportion to the degree of detachment from the world to which the soul has attained.'

Another figure of the Communion is offered by that touching scene after the Resurrection, when the two disciples, going towards Emmaus, and talking of 'all these things that had happened' met with our Lord. He noticed that they were sad and speaking of Him, and reassured them, saying, 'Ought not Christ to have suffered these things and so to enter into His glory?" Thus with the communicant, who, meditating those things that have happened, learns from such an example that suffering is necessary to enter into glory.

'We know it,' says F. Faber, speaking of the presence of Jesus—'we know it by a consciousness: that is, in addition to all the knowledge that sense, reason, and faith bestow upon us; we have also a knowledge which springs from hope, and from love and communion with Him.'

'The Council of Trent, with its wonderful and and unerring precision, has declared that our Saviour sits always at the right hand of the Father in heaven, according to the natural manner of existence, but that He is in many places sacramentally present with us by His substance, by that mode of existence, which, though it can scarcely be expressed in words, nevertheless, by the intellect illumined by faith, may be apprehended as possible with God. And what is this but what we read in the Gospel, when Jesus walked in another form with Cleophas and his fellow to Emmaus? They first knew Him not, and yet their hearts burned within them. Then the disciples constrained Jesus, saying, "Abide with us, for it is towards evening, and the day is now far spent".'

'Abide with us.' In the case of all indeed it may be said that 'the day is far spent'; for even with the young there is the uncertainty of life. He who makes such a request is certain to be heard; for we are told, 'Jesus went in with them'. And it was while He sat at table that He took bread and blessed it, and, breaking it, gave it to them. After which 'their eyes were opened and they knew Him'. Here it has been truly noted as remarkable that the disciples did not recognise our Lord until they had tasted the bread. 'It is then by Holy Communion that we receive the enlightment by which alone we can know our Lord and love Him. The soul that does not frequent Holy Communion will have a very imperfect and superficial knowledge of Him.' 'And He disappeared from before their eyes.' "Thus teaching us,' says the author of *Reflections and Prayers*, 'that the enjoyment of His sensible presence is not necessary to our act of thanksgiving.' 'Spiritual consolation is, as it were, a luminous trace that He has left of His presence, but it is not *He*, and it is *He* that we ought to love and to enjoy according to His will.'

'No one recognises Jesus,' says St. Bernard, 'save him who feels Him, and he that feels Him has hardly time to know Him, because He escapes almost as soon as He is felt.'

The 'Foolish' Virgins in the parable might have been 'good people,' who were associating with wise ones. As we know, the latter had brought oil for their lamps, but the former had been careless, and had made no provision; 'they all slumbered and slept. But at midnight a cry was heard, "Behold the Bridegroom cometh; go ye out to meet Him"— then all these Virgins rose and trimmed their lamps.'

It is remarkable how often the word 'foolishness,' not sin or guilt, is applied in the Scriptures, as it were with a sort of cynicism, to the proceedings of the complacent sinner. When the rich man was enjoying himself, and judgment impending, he was addressed as 'thou fool!' and this is surely the true judgment one is inclined to make, when we see some prosperous sinner complacently enjoying himself, with perhaps a smile of pity for the poor 'besotted' devotees who follow our Lord. Such apparent good sense is in reality the greatest 'foolishness' existing; and, stupidest of all, is your superior free-thinker.

'We may consider,' says the writer so often just quoted, 'the late arrival of the heavenly Bridegroom as signifying the delay of divine grace, which does not attract every soul at the same age or with equal strength. But it is necessary that we should always keep a clear conscience, that if Jesus should arrive suddenly, He may find nothing to offend Him in the state of our souls. In this sleep of the Virgins we may find a most striking image of the effect produced upon our souls by suffering a long interval to elapse between our communions. The soul which Jesus rarely enters becomes drowsy in the performance of its duties. At length it slumbers, and finally sinks into a profound sleep, in which the remonstrances of conscience can be no longer heard.'

The story goes on, with the significant announcement: 'They that were ready entered in with Him'. Those who approach careless and indifferent to the Holy Table, without oil, and sleeping without anxiety, hurry with their sisters to the feast, but find the 'door shut'. They did receive, but it is not the feast of the Bridegroom.

'Lord, Lord, open to us!' they cry, only to receive the cold answer, 'Verily, I know you not'. This sounds like the most awful rejection conceivable, and in that sense has been enforced from innumerable pulpits.

More remarkable is the account of the cure of the blind man Bartimeus, who, when he heard of our Lord's approach, called out, 'Have mercy on me!' and, when enjoined to silence, became even louder in his appeals. Thus should a soul impeded and uninterested set all impediments aside, and be only more persevering. The result was, we are told, 'that Jesus stood still'. His prayers had their effect. Our Lord is ready to listen, and to stand still, *nay, it is added*, 'He calleth thee'. The blind man 'cast off his mantle,' that is, put away all that could hinder his exertions, and ' came to Jesus'. Then this dialogue followed:

Jesus. 'What wilt thou that I should do to thee.'

The blind man. 'Lord, that I may receive my sight.'

Jesus. 'Go, thy faith hath healed thee.'

'Immediately he received his sight,' and we are then told that devout and grateful sufferer '*followed Him in the way*'.

So will those who are healed in the communion devoutly 'follow Him in the way'.

It is remarkable too that, when this blind man was clamouring for our Lord's aid, and certain intrusive persons charged him to hold his peace, 'he cried still louder'. 'So do friends and acquaintances, when the business and pleasant distractions of the world interpose, "charging us to hold our peace"; nay, who so much as ourselves, when every light excuse is caught at to put off or adjourn? In this case the blind man shows what ought to be done, which is only to "cry out louder," when Jesus will, of a surety, "stand still," and come to our aid.'

Another striking parable is found in the well-known scene with St. Thomas after the Resurrection. He, we are told, 'was not with the other disciples when Jesus came'. Thus, we can fancy that, when the faithful and pious are approaching the Holy Table, there may be one whose heart is not with the rest 'when Jesus comes'. It was strange, certainly, that one who had wished to die with our Lord should have been absent at this momentous crisis—our Lord's first appearance after all the agitating events of the Passion. Even as we read the story, there is something touching and dramatic in the lull and mystery of this moment. Naturally they said to Thomas in excitement that 'they had seen the Lord'. He had visited them. But this non-communicant had no such holy enthusiasm. He was incredulous.

He makes conditions. 'Unless I see in His hands the print,' &c. This sort of demand is well explained by the author of the *Reflections*. 'This boldness is a sign of secret unbelief, and the audacity of the desire betrays the absence of hope. And yet the Apostle had communicated in the upper chamber; and might not that mystery have prepared him to admit another? But a severe trial had followed his communion, and, as happens in many other cases, it had effaced the divine impression of the Holy Eucharist. How many prayers and mad desires we utter in the hearing of Jesus, in times of suffering, of adversity, even at the hour of communion! Thus St. Augustine says: 'For what do you ask, O mortal, since God has given you so much? . . . I desire at this moment to ask for more than Thomas required.' 'Eight days after,' the story goes on, 'the disciples were within, and Thomas with them. Jesus cometh, the doors being shut. He bade Thomas put his fingers into the print of the nails and his hand into the side.' Thus we see that, in spite of absence, coldness, doubts, denials, putting off, our Lord is ever ready to make the first advance. There can be no cause, therefore, for those who make the protest that they will be received ill. He is always ready, always inviting. "Be not faithless," He said, "but believing." I will make it easy for you.' This astonishing accessibility will, in truth, be one of the most fatal pieces of evidence against the half-worldling, whom it deprives of all excuse. No wonder it overpowered the doubting Apostle, who exclaimed, 'My Lord and my God!'

VI.

Prayers by the Saints and Others.

One of the most engaging characters in spiritual history is Sir Thomas More—now 'the Blessed'—who brought to his whole life and writings a simple practical spirit, that has an extraordinary charm for all sorts and conditions of men. Much of this was owing to his utter absence of *affectation;* he was so simple, straightforward; so unconsciously devoted to his profession, the exercise of which, conscientiously and to the best of his powers, he held to be true religion. No character, it may be said, is held in such sympathetic esteem by his countrymen.

Not long since, staying at an old country mansion and turning over the books in the library, I came upon a tiny black letter booklet—'a *lean* duodecimo,' as Sterne calls it—which I found to be one of his works, possibly but little known. It was called 'A Briefe Treatise to receive the Blessed Bodie of our Lord Saviour, sacramentally and virtually, both'. Quaint title!—and which is written in a direct lawyer-like spirit; kindly too, as if for the encouragement of those who, like himself, had to attend much to worldly things. The excellent Chancellor first thought of those who were disturbed by the sense of their own unfitness.

'I mean, not that any man is so good, or *can* be so good, that his goodness could make him worthy to receive into his vile, earthly body the holy, blessed Flesh and Blood of Almighty God . . . but that he may prepare himself, working with the grace of God, to stand in such state as the incomparable goodness of God will, of His liberal bounty, vouchsafe to take and accept for worthy to receive his own inestimable, precious Body into the body of *so simple a servant.* Such is the wonderful bounty of Almighty God that He not only doth vouchsafe, but also doth delight to be with men, if they prepare to receive Him *with honest and clean souls,* whereof He saith : " My delight and pleasures are to be with the sons of men ".

'In remembrance and memorial whereof He disdaineth not to take for worthy such men as wilfully make themselves not unworthy to receive the self-same blessed Body into their bodies, to the inestimable wealth of their souls ; and yet of His high and sovereign patience He refuseth not to enter bodily into the vile bodies of those whose filthy minds refuse to receive Him graciously into their souls.

'And, therefore, have we great cause with great dread and reverence to consider well the state of our own soul when we shall go to *the board of God, and as near as we can,* with help of His special grace, prayed for before, purge and clean our souls . . . lest that, if we presume so unreverently to receive this precious margaret, this pure pearl, the blessed Body of our Saviour Himself, that like a sort of swine, rooting in the dirt and wallowing in the ruin, we tread it under the filthy feet of our foul affections.'

How quaintly forcible the phrases of our good Chancellor—'*the board of God*'; 'as near as we can'; and 'so simple a servant'!

'For if we will but here consider, if there were a great worldly prince, which, for special favour that he bare us, would come visit us in our own house, what a business we would then make, and what a work it would be for us *to see that our house were trimmed up in every point to the best of our possible power*, and everything so provided and ordered that he should, by his honourable receiving, perceive what affection we have him, and in what high estimation we have him; we should by the comparing of that worldly prince and this heavenly Prince together (between which there is far far less comparison *than is between a man and a mouse*) inform and teach ourselves with how lowly mind, how tender and loving heart, how reverent, humble manner we should endeavour ourselves to receive this glorious heavenly King, the King of kings, Almighty God Himself, that so lovingly doth vouchsafe not only into our house, but His precious Body into our vile, wretched carcass, and His Holy Spirit into our poor, simple soul. What diligence can here suffice us? What solicitude can we think here enough against the coming of this Almighty King, coming for so special, gracious favour, not to put us to cost, not to spend of ours, but to enrich us of His?

'But, forasmuch as we neither can attain this great point of faith but by special grace of God, let us therefore pray for His gracious help, and for His help in the cleansing of our soul against His coming, that He make us worthy to receive Him worthily. And ever let us, *of our own part*, fear our own unworthiness, and, *of His part*, trust boldly upon His goodness, if we forslow not to work with Him for our own part. For if we willingly, upon the trust and comfort of His goodness, *leave our own devoir undone*, then is our hope no hope, but a very foul presumption.'

Without unduly deprecating the prayers of the popular manuals, it may be said that they are not all distinguished for purpose or vigour of utterance. Nay, there is often a certain varial unmeaningness, which is attempted to be supplied by repetitions, so that it is difficult in reaching the close to see what the intention is. However this may be, it is always well to choose the best when there is a choice; and these modern efforts cannot be put beside the nervous and pointed prayers written by the Saints, which 'mean business' in every line. A really good prayer should leave us in a different condition at the end to what we were at the opening. There should be reasoning, appeal to precedent, persuasion—topics which are different from the favourite models so often in use. To adopt the analogy of ordinary life, where an appeal is made for grace or favour to a superior, to make it effectual, the applicant should rest on such motives, as a course of previous favours and indulgence.

Prayer of St. Ambrose.

O great High Priest, Jesus Christ, who didst offer Thyself to God the Father, a pure and spotless victim, upon the altar of the cross, for us miserable sinners, and didst give us Thy Flesh to eat and Thy Blood to drink, ordaining that great mystery in virtue of Thy Holy Ghost; I entreat Thee by that same Blood of Thine, the great price of our salvation; I entreat Thee by that wonderful and unspeakable love wherewith Thou hast vouchsafed so to love us, miserable and unworthy, that Thou wouldst wash us from our sins in Thy Blood. Teach me, Thy unworthy servant, to approach so great a mystery with meek reverence and honour, such devotion and fear, as is fitting. Make me through Thy grace always so to believe and understand, to feel and firmly to hold concerning so great a mystery, which is pleasing to Thee and is good for my soul. May Thy good Spirit enter into my heart, and sound there without end.

Prayer of St. Ephraim.

Lord, who didst work so great a miracle at the pool of Siloam, in restoring to the blind man, not only the sight of his eyes, but the sight of his soul—for he proclaimed boldly that Thou wert his Physician, his Saviour, and his God; deign, Lord, to open our soul's eyes like his, so that we may be drawn to do Thy will with ardour. We are, in truth, far from the pool of Siloam: but we hold the chalice of Thy adorable Blood, full of brightness and life. Give us, through this chalice, the light and knowledge that is necessary for us to approach Thee with faith and fervour.

Prayer of Fénélon.

I feel, O my God, the truth and force of these words: 'It is hard to resist the spur'. Oh, how difficult it is to resist the interior attractions of Thy grace! Who has ever resisted Thee and found peace? Not only the impious and the worldling find no peace until they turn to Thee, but also the soul which Thou hast freed from the chains of sin cannot yet enjoy Thee, if by reserve or procrastination she still resists this sharp, piercing needle of Thy spirit, which urges her to an entire renunciation of self, to an interior death.

No, no, Lord, may I never for a single instant be opposed to Him who renders me good for evil. I detest my infidelities; even to the slightest imperfection, I reserve nothing. May all that can retard my sacrifice perish. It shall be no longer the to-morrow of a slothful soul ever deferring its conversion. To-day! to-day! What remains to me of life is not long enough for me to weep over my lost years. I say with Saul, Lord, what wouldst Thou have me to do? It seems to me as if I heard Thee replying: I will that thou love Me, and be happy in loving Me. Love and do what thou wilt, for in truly loving Me thou shalt only do what detached souls have done by pure love. Thou shalt love Me and make Me loved; thou shalt have no other will but Mine. By that My kingdom shall be established; by that I shall be adored in spirit and in truth; by that thou wilt sacrifice to Me the delights of sinful flesh and the pride of life; the entire world will no longer be anything to thee. Thou shalt no longer desire anything, that I alone may be all things to thee. Behold what I would have thee do. But how shall I do this, Lord? This work is above man's capacity. Ah! thou repliest in the depths of my heart, man of little faith, look at Saul, and doubt nothing. He says to thee, I can do all things in Him who strengthens me. He breathed but in the love of Jesus Christ. It was Jesus who lived triumphant in his Apostle, who was dead to all human things. Behold what God has done! The same hand can make thee what thou shouldst be also.

Prayer of St. Augustine.

To whom and how shall I tell of the profound abyss into which the weight of my concupiscence had dragged me, and of the sublime heights to which I have been ravished by the Spirit of love? To whom and how shall I tell it? Give thyself to me, O my God, for I love Thee, and if not enough, make me love Thee still more. I cannot measure how much is wanting to my love before it can satisfy Thee, so that my life may glide away in Thy embraces without ever falling back until it be hidden in the secret of Thy face.

All I know is, that in all besides Thee I find but misery, not only outside of myself, but within me, and that all abundance which is not my God is for me indigence. I will, then, love Thee, my God, because Thou hast first loved me, but where shall I find words to describe the proofs of Thy predilection, and Thy innumerable bounties in my regard? O fire ever burning and never decaying! O love always fervent and never growing cold! take possession of me, set me all on fire, that I may love Thee with all the powers of my soul. I love Thee, O my God, and burn to love Thee still more and more, for Thou surpassest the honey in sweetness and the sun in brightness.

Prayer of St. Augustine.

Almighty Father, who hast so loved the world as to give Thy only-begotten Son, that none who believe in Him should perish, but have everlasting life; by this Thy beloved Son, whose most holy Passion and glorious Resurrection and Ascension into heaven I commemorate, conduct, I beseech Thee, my soul out of prison, that it may praise Thy name.

Deliver me from the chains of my sins, and because my own deserts make me fear the condemnation of death, be appeased by the intercession of Thy beloved Son, and mercifully restore me to life. For what other mediator to send to Thee I know not, but Him who is the propitiation for our sins, who sits at Thy right hand making intercession for us, my Advocate with Thee the Father, the High Priest stained not with the blood of others, but His own ! A holy Victim, well-pleased and perfect, offered and accepted for an odour of sweetness; the Lamb without spot, who did no sin, but has borne our sins, and with His own bruises healed our infirmities. This is He whom Thou hast struck for the wickedness of Thy people, Thy beloved Son though He be, in whom Thou art well pleased.

Look, most gracious Father, on the Humanity of Thy beloved Son, and have pity on the infirmity of Thy weak creature. Behold the punishment of the Redeemer, and forgive the offence of the redeemed.

Make me, I beseech Thee, King of saints, by this Saint of saints, by this my Redeemer, to run the way of Thy commandments, that I may be united to Him in spirit who disdained not to be clothed in my flesh, Jesus Christ, blessed for ever. Amen.

Prayer of St. Thomas Aquinas.

Almighty and everlasting God, behold, I approach the Sacrament of Thy only-begotten Son our Lord Jesus Christ. I approach as one sick to the physician of life; as one unclean to the fountain of mercy; as one blind to the light of everlasting brightness; as one poor and needy to the Lord of heaven and earth. Therefore I implore the abundance of Thy measureless bounty, as far as Thou mayst vouchsafe to heal my infirmity, to cleanse my filth, to enlighten my blindness, to clothe my nakedness, that I may receive the Bread of Angels, the King of kings, and Lord of lords, with so much reverence and humility, so much contrition and devotion, so much purity and faith, such purpose and intention, as is expedient to my soul's salvation. Give me, I beseech Thee, to receive not only the Sacrament of the Lord's Body and Blood, but also the substance and efficacy of the Sacrament. O most gracious God! give me so to receive the Body of Thy only-begotten Son our Lord Jesus Christ, which He drew from the Virgin Mary, that I may merit to be incorporated with His mystical Body, and to be numbered among its members. O most loving Father, grant that I may at length perpetually contemplate His face revealed, Thy beloved Son, whom now I purpose to receive veiled on the way. Who lives and reigns with Thee. Amen.

Prayer of St. Thomas Aquinas after Communion.

I thank Thee, holy Lord, Almighty Father, everlasting God, because Thou hast vouchsafed to satisfy me, a sinner, Thy unworthy servant, for no merits of my own, but only by the condescension of Thy mercy, with the precious Body and Blood of Thy Son our Lord Jesus Christ. I entreat Thee that this holy communion may be to me not punishment for guilt, but a saving intercession for pardon. May it be to me the armour of faith and the shield of good will. May it be to me the evacuation of my faults, the extermination of concupiscence and lust, the augmentation of charity and patience, of humility and obedience; the strong defence against the snares of all my enemies, as well visible as invisible; the perfect quieting of my impulses, both carnal and spiritual; my firm adhesion to Thee, my one and true God; and the happy consummation of my end. And I pray Thee that Thou wouldst vouchsafe to bring me, a sinner, to that ineffable feast, where Thou, with Thy Son and the Holy Ghost, art to Thy saints true light, full contentment, everlasting joy, consummate pleasure, and perfect happiness. Through the same Christ. Amen.

Prayer of St. Bonaventure.

Transfix, most dear Lord Jesus, the marrow and heart of my soul with the most sweet and wholesome wound of Thy love, with the most holy charity, true, and serene, and apostolic, that my soul may swoon, and ever melt with the sole love and desire of Thee. Let it long and faint for Thy courts; let it wish to be dissolved and be with Thee. Give my soul to hunger for Thee, the Bread of Angels, the refreshment of holy souls, our daily supersubstantial Bread, which has all that is sweet in taste, and all that is delicious in sweetness. Let my heart ever hunger for Thee, and devour Thee, on whom the angels desire to look, and let the heart of my soul be filled with the sweetness of Thy taste. Let it ever thirst for Thee, the fountain of life, fountain of wisdom and knowledge, fountain of everlasting light, torrent of pleasure, and plenty of the house of God; let it ever canvass Thee, seek Thee, find Thee, go to Thee, arrive at Thee, meditate on Thee, talk of Thee, and do every work to the praise and glory of Thy name, with humility and discretion, with love and delectation, with readiness and affection, with perseverance even to the end. And be thou only always my hope, my whole confidence, my riches, my delight, my pleasure, my joy, my rest and tranquillity, my peace, my sweetness, my odour, my relish, my food, my refreshment, my refuge, my help, my wisdom, my portion, my possession, and my treasure, in which my soul and my heart may ever be fixed and firm, and immovably rooted. Amen.

Prayer of St. Augustine.

My God, my Creator, my support and nourishment, I hunger and thirst for Thee. For Thee my soul desires and sighs, and as a poor orphan at the bed of his parent who has just died embraces his cherished remains, weeping and sighing without ceasing, so Thy unworthy servant pours forth her tears in this sad exile at the remembrance of Thy Passion, Thy scourging, Thy wounds. So she sorrowfully reviews in her memory all the stages of Thy immolation, Thy taking down from the cross, and Thy burial, waiting as her only consolation with ardent desire for the glorious contemplation of Thy heavenly face.

O my Jesus, would to God that with the happy Joseph of Arimathea I had detached Thee from the cross, embalmed and laid Thee in the sepulchre, and that my feeble services had not been found wanting at such a funeral! O most mild, tender, and gentle Saviour, what reparation shall I make Thee, I who have not seen Thee clothed in corruptible flesh, who have not kissed the place of Thy wounds, the holes of the nails; I who have not watered with tears of gratitude these scars of Thy sacred Body? O adorable God, incomparable Saviour, how shalt Thou appease, how shalt Thou console my grief? No, it shall never cease to overwhelm me whilst I live exiled far from Thee.

Prayer of St. Augustine.

Pierce, O Lord, pierce, I implore Thee, my very hard heart with the very sweet and very powerful arrow of Thy love, and come from on high to penetrate by the power of Thy love to the most intimate corner of my being. Draw from my heart an ocean of tears, and a fountain of inexhaustible sobs. Let the warmth of Thy love and the longing to be admitted to Thy glories cause me to shed tears day and night. May I admit of no consolation during the days of my mortality until I merit to behold Thee on Thy heavenly throne, O most beautiful amongst the sons of men, my well-beloved Spouse, my Lord!

Prayers of Sir Thomas More.

I.

Glorious God! give me from henceforth the grace, with little respect unto the world, so to set and firmly fix mine heart upon Thee that I may say 'the world is crucified to me and I to the world. I desire to be dissolved and to be with Christ.' Give me the grace to amend my life, and to have an eye to mine end, without grudge of death, which to them that die in Thee, good Lord, is the gate of a wealthy life. O glorious God! all sinful fear, all sinful sorrow and pensiveness, all sinful hope, all sinful mirth and gladness take from me, Lord, that I may perform this thing most purely, to the everlasting glory of Thy name, to the honour of Thy most sweet Mother and Virgin, Mary, and to the honour of all Thy blessed saints and angels of heaven; to the soul health of me and to the souls' health of all Christian people, quick and dead.

II.

Lord, give us the grace to receive this blessed Body and Blood, this holy Soul, and this Almighty Godhead both into our bodies and into our souls, that the fruits of our good works may bear witness unto our consciences, that we receive Him worthily and in such a full faith and such a stable purpose of good living as we be bound to do. And then shall God give a gracious sentence, and say upon our soul, as He said upon Zaccheus, 'This day is health and salvation come into this house'; and that holy, blessed person of Christ, which we verily in the Blessed Sacrament receive, through the merit of His bitter Passion, whereof He hath ordained His own blessed Body in that Blessed Sacrament to be the memorial, vouchsafe, good Christian readers, to grant unto us all, and duly to thank Thee for Thy gracious visitation therewith, and at Thy high memorial, with tender compassions, to remember and consider Thy most bitter Passion.

Make us all, good Lord, virtuously participant of Thy Holy Sacrament this day; and every day make us all lively members, sweet Saviour Christ, of Thy holy Mystical Body, the holy Catholic Church. Do to me according to Thy great goodness.

III.

Good Lord, give me the grace in all my fear and agony to have recourse to that great fear and wonderful agony that Thou, my sweet Saviour, hadst at the Mount of Olives before Thy most bitter Passion, and in the meditation thereof to conceive ghostly comfort and consolation profitable to my soul.

Take from me, good Lord, this lukewarm fashion, or rather my cold manner of meditation and this dulness in praying to Thee, and give me warmth, delight, and guidance in thinking upon Thee: grant me the grace to long for Thy holy sacraments, and specially to rejoice in the presence of Thy very blessed Body, sweet Saviour Christ, in the Holy Sacrament of the Altar.

Prayer of Fenélon.

Jesus, eternal wisdom, hidden here in this Sacrament, I adore Thee this day. O blessed day, in which Thou gavest Thyself entire to the Apostles. To the Apostles do I say? Thou hast given Thyself no less to us than to them. Precious gift, renewed each day through so many centuries past, and which will last all days to the end of the world! O pledge of the goodness of the Father of Mercies! O Sacrament of Love! O supersubstantial Bread!— as my body is preserved by gross corruptible food, so should my soul be each day fed on the Eternal Truth, who not alone became flesh to be seen, but bread to be eaten, for the nourishment of the children of God.

O Lord, reject not my misery and iniquity! Under these poor veils Thou hidest the virtue and grandeur of Thy mystery. Here Thou wouldst exercise our faith; weak as I am, I deliver myself up to Thee; I can do nothing, but Thou art all powerful. I fear not my weakness when so near

Thee. Word of God! be with Thy weak creature as Thou art under the species of bread. O sovereign and living word, speak in the silence of my heart; let all be silent within me, that Thou mayest speak interiorly, and I listen but to Thee, O bread of life. I desire no other food but Thee alone; all other only feeds me with self and vain desires.

May my soul die the death of the just, that blessed death which should anticipate our corporal death; that interior death which separates the soul from self, wherein she no longer seeks nor desires, extinguishes anxious cares, destroys self-interest, and annihilates the love of all earthly things. O love, thou art a blissful torture. This celestial bread, descending from heaven, makes us both live and die; it tears the soul from itself and places it in peace. It takes all and gives all—takes all of self, and gives all of God, in whom all things are pure. O my love, my life, my all, I desire none but Thee. O my heavenly bread, on Thee may I daily feed, and only dread to lose Thee.

Prayer of Bourdaloue.

Lord, no one can come to Thee unless Thou drawest him. You see the hardness of my heart, and Thou canst soften it. In one instant Thou canst melt all that ice which makes it so cold and indifferent to Thee. A single ray of Thy grace will do it. I know, my God, how little am I entitled to that intimate connection with which Thou dost privilege certain chosen souls at Thy altar. Let me but feel some of those interior inspirations, those burning lights which transport them out of themselves. Must I ever be in Thy presence as a dry clod of earth? ever slow and torpid when I am to approach Thy Holy Table? Draw me after Thee. If I now pray Thee to change my heart, it is that it may be bound for ever to Thee, may never turn from Thee, and enjoy no pleasure but what is found in Thee. My happiness in this life is to possess Thee in the shape of these frail emblems.

It is for sinners, O my God, as well as for the just, that Thy Sacrament was instituted. Adorable Saviour! when Thou wert upon earth, Thou condescendedst to eat at the sinner's table; now, in the same spirit, Thou admittest penitent sinners to Thy Table; and, as formerly Thou didst sit at the table of the sinner converted by Thy grace, more joyfully than at that of the haughty Pharisee, so there is no one more gladly welcomed by Thee than the sinners who renounce their sins to come to Thee.

A Devout Prayer to Jesu.

(From the Sarum Hours, 1508.)

O glorious Jesu, O meekest Jesu, O most sweetest Jesu, I pray Thee that I may have true confession, contrition, and satisfaction or I die; and that I may see and receive Thy holy Body, God and man, Saviour of all mankind, Christ Jesu, without sin; and that Thou wilt, my Lord God, forgive me all my sins for Thy glorious wounds; and that I may end my life in the true faith of Holy Church; and I commend my soul to Thy holy hands, through the glorious help of Thy Blessed Mother of Mercy, our Lady Saint Mary, and all the holy company of heaven.

The holy Body of Christ Jesu be my salvation of body and soul. Amen.

The glorious Blood of Christ Jesu bring my soul and body to everlasting bliss. Amen.

I cry, God mercy! I cry, God mercy! I cry, God mercy! Welcome, my Maker! Welcome, my Redeemer! Welcome, my Saviour! I cry Thee mercy, with heart contrite of my great unkindness that I have had to Thee!

O the most sweetest Spouse of my soul, Christ Jesu, desiring heartily ever more for to be with Thee in mind and will, and to let no earthly thing be so nigh my heart as Thou, Christ Jesu; and that I may evermore say to Thee, with a glad cheer: My Lord, my God, my Sovereign Saviour, Christ Jesu! I beseech Thee heartily take me, sinner, unto Thy great mercy and grace; for I love Thee with all my heart, with all my mind, and with all my might; and nothing so much in earth or above earth, as I do Thee, my sweet Lord, Christ Jesu. And for that I have not loved Thee, and worshipped Thee above all things, as my Lord, my God, and Saviour, Christ Jesu, I beseech Thee, with meekness and heart contrite, mercy and forgiveness of my great unkindness, and for the great love that Thou sheddest for me and all mankind, what time Thou offeredst Thy glorious Body, God and man, unto the Cross, there to be crucified and wounded, and into Thy glorious heart a sharp spear, there running out plenteously blood and water for the redemption and salvation of me and all mankind, and thus having remembrance steadfastly in myne heart of Thee, my Saviour, Christ Jesu.

I doubt not but Thou wilt be full nigh me and comfort me both bodily and ghostly with Thy glorious presence, and at the last bring me into Thy everlasting bliss, which shall never have end. Amen.

The Prayer from the Office of the Holy Cross.
(Translated by Crashaw.)

O my Lord Jesu Christ, Son of the living God, interpose, I pray Thee, Thine own precious death, Thy Cross and Passion, betwixt my soul and Thy judgment, now and in the hour of my death. And vouchsafe to grant me Thy grace and mercy; to the living and dead, remission and rest; to Thy Church, peace and concord; to us, sinners, life and glory everlasting.

Orison : "Deus cui proprium".
(From the Prymer, 1400.)

God, to whom it is proper to be merciful and to spare evermore, underfong (undertake) our prayers; and the mercifulness of Thy pity assoil him that the chain of trespass bindeth. By Christ our Lord. So be it.

Prayer of St. Theresa.

Blessed be Thou, O my Saviour, who to love us asketh nothing but to be loved by us.

VII.
L'Envoi.

As we began this little tract with the thought of the Tabernacle, so shall we end it. Kings and potentates have their palaces; but in every corner of the earth there is the palace of the King of kings, where He lives, and watches, and receives His subjects, ever accessible, ever present,—our friend and companion, one of the millions of living beings who are upon the earth. The presence of so august a guest should fill—

> ' All thoughts, all passions, all delights;
> Whatever stirs this mortal frame,'

and turn all eyes, at all hours and in every action, to the Tabernacle. 'The best way of making a communion,' says F. Dupont, in his *Meditations*, 'is to think that it is to be the very last—a sort of Viaticum,' and in this sense he applies a striking passage from the Wise Man: 'When you have sat down to eat at the table of the Prince, diligently consider what is placed before you, *and putting a knife to your throat*,' that is, as though the next moment was to be your last. As Cardinal Newman says—

> ' Christ Himself for food be given,
> Faith become the cup of heaven
> Out of which the joy is quaffed
> Of the Spirit's sobering draught.

> ' With that joy replenished,
> Morn shall glow with modest red,
> Noon with beaming faith be bright,
> Eve be soft without twilight.'

This divine food is marked with the memorable sign, 'in which thou shalt conquer,' and which the same writer sings:

'THE SIGN OF THE CROSS.

'Whene'er across this sinful flesh of mine
   I draw the holy sign,
All good thoughts stir within me, and renew
   Their slumbering strength divine ;
Till there springs up a courage, high and true,
   To suffer and to do.'

There are a number of works on the Holy Communion—all no doubt excellent—but among these there are some of special value, and these, according to the fate of such cases, are not so well known. There is, of course, the familiar Fourth Book of *The Imitation*. Next we have the ever-charming *Introduction to a Devout Life*, with which James I. was so delighted that he declared its author was 'a true saint,' and sent him an invitation to visit him. A remarkable body of thought and piety is the *Reflections and Prayers*, abundantly suggestive, a work warmly commended by Cardinal Manning as 'in a high degree real and solid. Not only in language, but in the train of thought, it is truthful, and gives utterances to the spiritual acts which are common to persons of a devout life. Devotional works are often far-fetched, so to speak, in two ways: some are imaginative, and remote from our ordinary and healthy experience; others are so elevated and exceptional in the supernatural life that we cannot make them our own. The present volume is throughout both practical and proximate to our daily needs.' In addition, it is singularly interesting. For a small treatise, embracing the whole subject in every point of view, there is scarcely anything so satisfactory as the *Traité de la Communion* of the Jesuit, P. Vaubert. Of another sort, and remarkable for the variety of the thoughts and suggestions as well as for its scriptural tone, is *La Nouvelle Année Eucharistique*. Finally, there is the admirable *Preparation for Death* by S. Alphonsus Liguori, every page of which is practical, businesslike, and to the point. This also is highly scriptural.* Thus equipped, the pious Christian may go his way instructed, comforted, and rejoicing.

It were to be wished that some pious person should select the best known prayers and meditations—that is to say, those nervous, solid, and *compelling* prayers, by which heaven is, as it were, taken by violence.

The excellent Dr. Johnson, who was Catholic in all but name, said shortly before his death, that he had thought of forming a Book of Prayers, selecting the best known. When his friends importuned him to undertake the work, he grew agitated and said, 'Do not talk thus of what is so awful! I know not what time God will allow me in this world. Let me alone; I am overpowered.' He then covered his hands and reclined for some time upon the table. The Doctor had the pious habit of consecrating every act of his day by a written prayer for direction, thus 'casting his cares upon Him who hath care of us'.

What an epitome of solid, practical piety is in his nervous lines:

> 'Still raise for good the supplicating voice,
> But leave to Heaven the measure and the choice;
> Safe in His hands whose eye discerns afar
> The secret ambush of a specious prayer.
> Implore His aid—in His decisions rest;
> Secure whate'er He gives, He gives the best.

---

* To these may be added Pere Dupont's *Meditations*, highly recommended to me by a friend of much knowledge, piety, and reading in this direction.

> But when a sense of Sacred Presence fires,
> And strong devotion to the skies aspires,
> Pour forth thy fervours for a healthful mind,
> Obedient passions, and a will resigned ;
> For love, which scarce collective man can fill ;
> For patience, sovereign o'er transmuted will ;
> For faith that, panting for a purer seat,
> Counts death kind nature's signal for retreat—
> These gifts for all the laws of Heaven ordain,
> These gifts He grants who grants the power to gain ;
> With these celestial wisdom calms the mind,
> And makes the happiness she cannot find.'

Without this firm purpose, life is but a fitful uncertain play. As an old writer has it, 'to be alone it grieveth us ; to be accompanied it troubleth us ; to live long it wearieth us ; and sufficient contenteth us not'. With the Tabernacle there is neither solitude, nor intrusive company, nor the encumbrance of time, nor discontent. And so, to conclude, with these burning words of St. Ambrose sounding in our ears : ' This is the bread of life, who eats of it therefore cannot die ; for how can he die whose sustenance is *Life ?* And how can he, who holds this life-giving substance, fail ? Draw near, then, and refresh yourselves, for it is bread. Draw near and drink, for it is a fountain. Draw near and you shall have light, for this is a light. Draw near and you shall be free, for where the spirit of God is, there is freedom. Draw near and you shall have pardon, for it is the remission of sins. You ask what is this bread, and our Lord tells you Himself, " I am the Bread of Life, who comes to Me shall not hunger, and who believes in Me shall not thirst ".'

With which, indulgent reader, I take my leave, heartily echoing the wish of good Sir Thomas More, on the day before his execution, 'So may we all meet *merrily* in heaven ! '

www.ingramcontent.com/pod-product-compliance
Lightning Source LLC
Chambersburg PA
CBHW020304090426
42735CB00009B/1210